The
Effective
President

The Effective President

Edited by
John C. Hoy
Melvin H. Bernstein

University of California, Irvine

Palisades Publishers
Pacific Palisades, California

Library of Congress Catalog Card Number: 76-17928

International Standard Book Numbers:
0-913530-5-0 (paper)
0-913530-06-9 (cloth)

Palisades Publishers
P.O. Box 744, Pacific Palisades, California 90272

Printed in the United States of America

Contents

Preface

The Effective President was born out of the Symposium on
the American Presidency held at the University of California,
Irvine, at the outset of the nation's Bicentennial Year. Because
of the originality and thoughtfulness of the addresses delivered at
the Symposium, it is our particular pleasure to be able to present
them now in essay form to a broader audience.

The Symposium was designed to bring political science
students and faculty from more than 40 colleges and universities
together with public leaders, journalists, writers, and scholars of
national renown for three days of intense discussions on the issues
associated with effective leadership in the nation's highest
office. These commentaries, forward looking yet with an
historical perspective, offer rich and varied insight by thinkers
with immense and broad experience in the study of the
Presidency. They provide an unusual opportunity to take an
in-depth look at the meaning and significance, the problems and
prospects for Presidential leadership at a most critical time in our
nation's history. The essays stand alone yet all relate to the
central theme of effective leadership. In cases where questions
and answers or commentary and responses follow the essays they
have been carefully selected from the wealth of such material
discussed at the Symposium and have been printed virtually
verbatim for purposes of spontaneity.

We are profoundly grateful to several organizations and individuals who made the UCI Symposium possible and who also provided the support necessary to accomplish the editing and publication of the proceedings. These notable individuals represent a broad range of political persuasion yet all have revealed deep interest in the discussion and debate of major public policy issues: Walter B. Gerken, Chairman of the Board, Pacific Mutual Life Insurance Company; Raymond Watson, President, the Irvine Company; Preston Hotchkis, Sr.; Charles Ferguson, President, AVCO Financial Insurance Group; Roy Ash; Robert L. Flynne, Chairman of the Board and Chief Executive Officer, Smith-International, Inc.; Patrick F. Cadigan, President, Electronic Engineering Company of California; William Laughlin, Chairman of the Board of the Saga Administrative Corporation; and Mrs. Fred Harber. In addition, Charles Thomas, former Secretary of the Navy under President Eisenhower; Joseph Cerrell, President of Cerrell Associates; Jack Calkins of the White House Staff; Professor James Lare of Occidental College and President of the Southern California Center for Education in Public Affairs, Dr. Gordon Hoxie, President of the Center for the Study of the Presidency; and Christian Werner, Dean, School of Social Sciences, UCI, were of great help in providing the guidance that led to development of the original program.

We also are indebted to James Roosevelt, Professor Barbara Stone, and Dr. Joel Fisher for skillful moderation of their respective panels on public opinion, Presidential leadership, and White House-Congressional relations. Mr. Roosevelt, a long-time observer of the Washington scene, has been a Congressman, a Democratic National Committeeman, and presently is a Lecturer on Congress in the Program on Social Ecology at the University of California, Irvine. Professor Stone, author of various books and articles on government, is Chairperson of the Political Science Department, California State University, Fullerton. Dr. Fisher, an active public speaker and writer on American foreign policy and international relations, has served as both a United States State Department officer and a member of the White House staff.

Finally, the editors express their deepest appreciation to the following staff at UCI who contributed so much to the success of the Symposium and publication of the proceedings: Marie Vance, Toby Milligan, Margaret Hernandez, Janet Mosk, and Linda Watkins. Lance Robbins, Student Coordinator for UCI and Associate Editor of the *New University* campus newspaper, also provided valuable assistance in arranging for the Symposium.

The Effective President represents the first effort by the University of California, Irvine, in developing a comprehensive publication emerging from one of the major public affairs programs sponsored by the ten-year-old campus.

J.C.H.
M.H.B.

Contributors

JOHN B. ANDERSON, U.S. Representative from Illinois since
1960, is Chairman of the House Republican Conference and
meets regularly with President Ford. He is the second-ranking
Republican member of the Rules Committee and the ranking
Republican member on the Joint Committee on Atomic Energy.
He also serves as a member of the Republican Policy Committee
and Research Committee and was a delegate to the Republican
National Convention in 1972. Prior to his election to Congress,
he was a faculty member of Northeastern University School of
Law, State's Attorney of Winnebago County, Illinois, and a
member of the U.S. State Department Career Diplomatic
Service. He is the author of *Vision and Betrayal in America*
(1975) and *Between Two Worlds: A Congressman's Choice*
(1970). He has law degrees from Harvard Law School and the
University of Illinois, from which he graduated Phi Beta Kappa.

MELVIN H. BERNSTEIN is a political scientist and an attorney who
is Assistant Vice Chancellor for Educational Relations at the
University of California, Irvine, and lecturer in law and politics
at its School of Social Sciences. He has written articles on
government and politics for *New Republic, Nation, California*

Journal, Forum, and the *Sacramento Bee.* Dr. Bernstein is Vice President and General Counsel of the Southern California Center for Education in Public Affairs, past Chairman of the Arts and Sciences Committee of the Republican State Central Committee of California, and served as Chairman of the Advisory Committee to the California Republican Platform Convention in 1974.

DOUGLASS CATER is Director of the Aspen Institute Program on Communications and Society and Consulting Professor at Stanford University. He served as Special Assistant to President Lyndon B. Johnson, concentrating on education and health programs, and in 1967-68 as Secretary to the Cabinet. He also has been a consultant to the Secretary of the Army, Secretary of State, and the Director of Mutual Security. Mr. Cater is the author of *Power in Washington* (1964) and *The Fourth Branch of Government* (1959) and formerly was Washington editor and national affairs editor of *The Reporter Magazine.*

THOMAS CRONIN is author of *The State of the Presidency* (1975) and coauthor of a widely used text on American politics, *Government by the People* (1975). A former White House Fellow, Dr. Cronin has been an adviser to cabinet members, Congressional committees, and the U.S. Civil Service Commission. Currently Visiting Professor of Politics at Holy Cross College and Brandeis University, he has written cover-story essays for *Saturday Review, Washington Monthly,* and *Commonweal.* He is a frequent contributor to the Los Angeles *Times* and numerous academic journals. He is editor and coauthor of *The Presidency Reappraised* (1974) and *The Presidential Advisory System* (1969).

GRANT DILLMAN has been Vice President and Washington, D.C., Manager of United Press International since 1970. He first joined the wire service in 1942 in Columbus, Ohio, where he was State House reporter. After promotion to Washington, he was assigned to the House of Representatives and reported on the House Committee on Unamerican Activities. In 1950 he assumed responsibility for the UP Washington Report for morning newspapers and since 1948 has covered every national political convention. He is Chairman of the National Freedom of Information Committee of Sigma Delta Chi, a society of professional journalists, and a member of the National Press Club, Washington Press Club, and the Gridiron Club.

MERVIN D. FIELD is the founder of the Field Research Corporation, one of the nation's largest consumer and opinion research organizations. He also inaugurated *The California Poll,* a continuing media-sponsored service reporting on the public's response to candidates, election issues, and a variety of social problems and concerns. A director of the Roper Public Opinion Research Center at Williams College, he also is a trustee of the National Council of Published Polls and a member of the New York Market Research Council and the Executive Council of the American Association for Public Opinion Research.

GEORGE GALLUP, JR., former Editor of *The Gallup Poll,* has served as its President since 1966. He is the coauthor of a soon-to-be published book on the 1972 presidential campaign and author of numerous articles on voting behavior of various population groups, urban affairs, and polling methods. A director of the Roper Public Opinion Research Center at Williams College, he is a member of both the American and World Associations of Public Opinion Research. He also serves on the Advisory Council of the Department of Sociology of Princeton University and as a director of Religion in American Life, Inc.

STEPHEN HESS is a Senior Fellow in Governmental Studies at the

Brookings Institution. The views expressed in his essay are solely his and should not be attributed to the Institution. He served as Deputy Assistant to the President for Urban Affairs in 1969 and as National Chairman for the White House Conference on Children and Youth, 1969-71. He is author of *The Presidential Campaign: An Essay on the Leadership Selection Process after Watergate* (1974) and coauthor of *Nixon: A Political Portrait* (1969), *The Republican Establishment: The Present and Future of the G.O.P.* (1967) and *Hats in the Ring: The Making of Presidential Candidates* (1960). Dr. Hess is a frequent commentator on radio and television both in the United States and abroad and has written articles for such national publications as *Atlantic Monthly, Harper's,* and *U.S. News and World Report.*

STEPHEN HORN is President of California State University, Long Beach, and has had an extensive career in public affairs. He was Administrative Assistant to former Secretary of Labor James P. Mitchell and later was Legislative Assistant to U.S. Senator Thomas H. Kuchel. He currently serves as Vice Chairman of the U.S. Commission on Civil Rights, and was a member of the President-Elect's Task Force on Organization of the Executive Branch following the 1968 election. He also was a member of the Department of Housing and Urban Development's Urban Studies Fellowship Advisory Board and the Department of Justice's National Advisory Committee on Law Enforcement Education Program. Dr. Horn is author of *The Cabinet and Congress* (1960) and *Unused Power: The Work of the Senate Committee on Appropriations* (1970).

JOHN C. HOY is Vice Chancellor for University Affairs and Student Affairs at the University of California, Irvine, Senior Lecturer at the Graduate School of Administration, and Senior Fellow in the University Studies Program. He has authored and coauthored several books, has published articles for the *Saturday*

Review, Christian Science Monitor, and *National Observer,* and has had a syndicated column for 350 newspapers through the Newspaper Enterprises Association of New York City. Mr. Hoy is a member of the Board of Educators for the Center for the Study of the Presidency, and has served as consultant to various governmental committees such as the United States Senate Subcommittee on Education and the Joint Legislative Committee for the Revision of the California Master Plan for Higher Education.

HUBERT H. HUMPHREY was the first Democrat to be elected United States Senator from Minnesota, and served in that office from 1949 to 1964 when he was elected as the 38th Vice President of the United States. Two years after being defeated by Richard Nixon in the 1968 Presidential election by less than one-half of one percent of the vote, he returned to the U.S. Senate. He is Chairman of the Foreign Relations Committee, the Joint Economic Committee, and the Consumer Economic Subcommittee and serves as a member of several other committees and subcommittees of the Senate. He is author of *The Political Philosophy of the New Deal* (1970), *Beyond Civil Rights* (1968), *The Cause is Mankind* (1964) and *War on Poverty* (1964). Mr. Humphrey's legislative work presently includes world food shortage, modernization of Congress, election and campaign reforms, rural and urban development, and civil rights.

LOUIS KOENIG is Professor of Political Science at New York University and has authored two books on the Presidency, *The Chief Executive* and *The Invisible Presidency.* He also is coauthor of *The Presidency Today.* Dr. Koenig serves as Consultant to the Bureau of the Budget of the United States State Department and has been a member of the National Resources Planning Board. In addition, he has had a thoughful series on the Presidency for CBS television.

KARL LAMB is author of *As Orange Goes: Twelve California Families and the Future of American Politics* (1974), and Professor of Politics and Fellow at Cowell College at the University of California, Santa Cruz. He also is coauthor of *Congress: Politics and Practice* and *Campaign Decision-Making*. A former Rhodes Scholar at Oxford, Dr. Lamb was a member of the political science faculty at the University of Michigan.

ROBERT D. NOVAK is a former Chief Congressional Correspondent for *The Wall Street Journal*, and now writes with Rowland Evans, Jr. the Washington column "Inside Report" that is syndicated in more than 250 newspapers in the United States and abroad. He has been on the editorial staffs of several midwest newspapers and the Capitol Hill Correspondent for the Associated Press. Mr. Novak is the coauthor of *Nixon in the White House* (1971), *Lyndon B. Johnson: The Exercises of Power* (1966), and *The Agony of the G.O.P.* (1964). He has written both alone and in collaboration with Mr. Evans for *Esquire, The New Republic, The National Observer,* and other magazines.

NELSON W. POLSBY is Professor of Political Science at the University of California, Berkeley. He served as a member of the Democratic National Committee's Commission on Vice Presidential Selection in 1973-74. Dr. Polsby is author of *The Modern Presidency* (1973), *Congressional Behavior* (1971), *Presidential Elections* (1971) and coauthor of *Congress and the Presidency* (1964). From 1963-65, he was a member of the General Advisory Committee of the U.S. House of Representatives Select Committee on Government Research.

GEORGE E. REEDY is Dean and Nieman Professor at the College of Journalism, Marquette University, and served as Press Secretary and Special Assistant to President Lyndon B. Johnson, 1964-66.

A former Washington correspondent for United Press and reporter for the *Phildelphia Inquirer*, he is author of *The Presidency in Flux* (1973), *The Twilight of the Presidency* (1970) and *Who Will Do Our Fighting for Us?* (1969). He also has contributed political and journalistic articles to the *New York Times, New Republic,* and *Nation,* and has taught courses at Northwestern University School of Journalism and State University of New York. He served as a director of the Business-Government Relations Council and as a member of the President's Advisory Commission on Selective Service.

GERALD WARREN is editor of the *San Diego Union.* He was appointed in 1969 as Deputy Press Secretary to the President with responsibility for directing the news operation in the White House. During most of 1973 and through August, 1974, he was the principal briefing officer. He continued as Deputy Press Secretary during the first year of the Ford Administration with responsibility for maintaining liaison with editors, publishers, and broadcasters. He formerly served as a reporter with the *Lincoln* (Neb.) *Star,* business representative for Copely News Service, and City Editor and Assistant Managing Editor for the *San Diego Union.*

AARON WILDAVSKY is Dean of the Graduate School of Public Policy at the University of California, Berkeley, and coauthor of *Presidential Elections* (1971) and editor of the books, *The Presidency* (1969), *U.S. Foreign Policy: Perspectives and Proposals for the 1970's* (1969), and *American Governmental Institutions* (1968). He is a consultant to the U.S. Department of Justice and an executive member of the Assembly of Behavioral and Social Sciences of the National Academy of Sciences. He also is a member of the Resources Development Advisory Group of the U.S. Army Institute for the Behavioral and Social Sciences.

1

Introduction: The Contradictions of Presidential Leadership

John C. Hoy and *Melvin H. Bernstein*

The recent crisis of confidence that pervades the Presidency is but a part of the overall public disillusionment with major institutions and leaders throughout American society at a time of unremitting change and controversy. Abuses of Executive power culminating in the cataclysm of Watergate present us with the profound dilemma of redefining the purposes of Presidential leadership as we enter the third century of the history of the Republic. James Madison in effect defined the problem for us when he wrote to Thomas Jefferson on October 17, 1788, "It is a melancholy reflection that liberty should be equally exposed to danger whether the Government has too much or too little power." If we take a longer, more historical view of Watergate, one wonders whether overdocumentation of the "crisis" has led to a loss of perspective on the real meaning of the Presidency, that flexible, adaptive institution found in the world's oldest democratic constitutional document.

THE QUEST FOR A NATIONAL SENSE OF COMMUNITY

Beginning with the early 1960's the national consensus that is required for effective leadership quickly began to fragment and eventually erupted into civil disorders by the end of the decade. Factional conflict appeared as the order of the day while some leaders searched for support from a loosely defined "silent majority" of the American people. George Reedy, one of the most perceptive writers of the Presidency of the past decade, contends that national consensus or a strong sense of community among the American people must be restored before we can again expect decisive leaders to appear who will re-unite the country and set it once again on a purposeful course. As Reedy puts it, "Leadership is a function of the interaction between politicians who are trying to get power, trying to lead society, and constituents who are looking for leadership. When we do get those leaders there is some sort of catalytic arrangement that brings the two together. But when we don't get such leaders, what is really happening to us is that our society has reached a stage where it is not prepared for decisive leadership."

On the one hand, absence of a national sense of community and prevalence of sectional strife was found at the onset of the Civil War in 1861. On the other hand, national consensus for action supported the leadership of Theodore Roosevelt in acting against the ills of an emerging industrialized society, Woodrow Wilson in taking the country into World War I, and Franklin Roosevelt in first unifying the nation through the upheavals of the Great Depression and then leading a committed people through the trials of the Second World War.

The present lack of cohesion in American society is reflected in the existing tension between the Executive and Congress forcing a deadlock or stalemate over vital policy issues in the areas of energy, the environment, taxation, health care, and transportation. Congressman John Anderson of Illinois warns that sharp disagreements between the Executive and Congressional branches of national government over critical issues in foreign policy, national security, and domestic affairs have reached the point where legislative checks against Presidential initiatives have become excessive and even counterproductive. When conflict rather than compromise prevails as the mode of operation in our federal government where opposition political parties control the White House and the Congress, it becomes questionable whether the requisite unity of purpose can be established that characterizes the actions of great nations.

ATTITUDES OF AMERICAN VOTERS

While the Watergate scandal and its exposition thoroughly demoralized public trust in the White House, it is telling to observe how President Ford's deliberate efforts to clean up the mess and present himself as an honest, straightforward man of the people have largely been met by renewed public confidence in the Presidency as a central institution of American society. Contrary to popular thinking, just one year after Nixon's resignation, a Gallup Poll found that the Presidency/Executive Branch commands more public confidence than either the United States Congress or the United States Supreme Court, with a majority of those surveyed expressing at least "quite a lot" of confidence in the Presidency. Also it is revealing that even at the height of Watergate, instead of the apathy and discontent with politics expected as the attitude of youth, student leaders surveyed on college and university campuses in California agreed that citizens must become more politically involved, politicians must win the people's trust, and that they as campus activists would actively pursue careers in public life to remedy what they see as abuses of the political process.

It is clear from this book, particularly the contributions of Mervin Field, George Gallup, Jr., and Karl Lamb, that youth does not vote as a monolithic and idealistic bloc but reflects more pragmatic factors such as whether in or out of college, parental influence, socioeconomic status, candidate personality appeal, and concrete issues of the campaign. Practical influences on the vote of youth were illustrated dramatically during the 1972 Presidential campaign when the youth vote came close to evenly dividing between the two candidates despite George McGovern's carefully constructed strategy to win major support among young people while Richard Nixon hoped at best for a fair share of their votes. The actual youth vote in the seventies is more pragmatic and realistic than its much publicized anti-establishment counterpart of the 1960's. George Gallup, Jr., notes that, "Our youth today are further turned off by the traditional type of politicking. People want openness and directness in candidates—character not charisma." In particular, the current generation of campus activists, highly motivated toward public life, represents the potential of the next generation of leadership in the country. The dismal experience of sweeping White House corruption evoked a kind of counter-reaction from leaders in Congress and the Judiciary who rose to the demands occasioned by the constitutional crisis produced. Campus leaders appear more realistic as well as skeptical now about the limitations as well as the potential of active political engagement. It can be expected that since they do represent the largest age cohort of college and university students in the nation's history, the output of a relatively recently expanded system of universal higher education, they will certainly be heard from in a significant way in the political future of their society.

Although special issues such as Watergate and election reform, race relations and bussing, and violent crime capture the public's attention from time to time the overriding concerns for peace and prosperity are dominant in Presidential election years. Currently American global influence relative to the intricacies of detente, coupled with the problems of inflation and unemployment related to the maintenance of a healthy economy, prevail as the top concerns of most American voters.

The qualities Americans prefer in their President seem tailored to contemporary developments but in fact are consistent with the Field and Gallup polls of recent decades. Voters look for candidates who are strong, in touch with public feelings, smart but not too complex, who can motivate and inspire people. An honest, "take charge" leader is one who receives public approval while voters react negatively to Presidents who come across as dishonest, deceitful, isolated from the people, who vacillate about decisions and seem unable to take command of the country. The polls show the American people will make temporary sacrifices and face up to necessary hardships in order to preserve the base line desire for a high standard of living and democratic way of life. The people are further prepared to use the economic and military power of this nation to preserve and protect American interests here and abroad when the issues are presented forthrightly.

The late Walter Lippmann summed it up well when he wrote that the President must deal with the American people seriously, truthfully, responsibly, and squarely, "They are asked to put their trust in the President, which indeed they must, for he is the President; but in return they must have his trust and they must have his confidence and they must have his guidance." A delicate balance obviously has to be drawn between the competing interests of secrecy and disclosure, but a Presidential leader runs a great risk if he cannot convince the American people he is leveling with them.

THE POSSIBILITIES AND PROBLEMS OF DIVIDED GOVERNMENT

The American political system of checks and balances and shared powers is difficult enough to govern effectively when one of the two major political parties controls both the White House and the Congress. However, when as in fifteen of the past twenty-two years, the Presidency and Congress have been held by the opposition parties at the same time, divided government impedes if not prevents united, purposeful leadership where a single party in power can be held accountable for its management of the nation's affairs. Still, as Robert Novak contends, the frequency of this arrangement over two decades indicated that divided government is the will of the American people and serves as a useful and effective check against executive excesses of a President such as Richard Nixon bent on manipulating the power of government to his personal political philosophy even though it violates both the spirit and letter of the Constitution.

Novak further argues that recent conflict between executive and legislative branches, whether involving a Lyndon Johnson or a Richard Nixon, is a healthy condition in itself. He points out:

> Actually, the original function of the Congress, I believe, as set forth in the Constitution of the United States, was not to rubber stamp and not to automatically approve the program of a President, not to be a bill-passing machine because a parliamentary system could well serve that purpose, but to serve as an independent branch and perhaps to operate in a direction counter to the President. Indeed if there had been more conflict between Lyndon Johnson and the 89th Congress, the good that might have been accomplished, both domestically and foreign, could have been immense.

Setting realistic expectations for American Presidents requires recognition of the fact that leadership on the vital questions of our time must come from all levels of society, particularly the organized institutions of local and state government as well as universities, churches, civic groups, and industry. The opportunities for effective leadership in such a pluralistic society operating with a politically divided government are dramatically limited and we must above all else realize that our Presidents cannot be all things to all people. Despite the rhetoric, grandeur, and power of the Office, the President is human and subject to many of the same fears, anxieties, eccentricities, and moods as the rest of us, yet he alone is obligated to decide and act.

CONSTRAINTS ON RATIONAL PLANNING IN THE WHITE HOUSE

Modern methods of management, organization, and executive leadership may be applicable to many institutions in our technological society, but for the Presidency we must remember that this is essentially a political office that leaves little room for the niceties of rational planning. First of all, special political skills and techniques such as coalition building are needed to win Presidential campaigns. Campaign skills, however, are not necessarily related to the abilities needed to exercise Presidential leadership and to administer effectively the executive branch of national government. Promises made and appointments pledged during the heat of a campaign have little to do with developing sound policies and making wise selections of people to serve in federal institutions and manage the agencies of government.

Even the most ideal programs will fail of adoption unless the President has enough clout to carry his initiatives through Congress or the skill to negotiate compromises with those whom he shares power over legislation. What begins as an ideal proposal on taxes, energy, or the environment may result in a bill that is partially watered down but at least becomes timely legislation.

A President must retain flexibility in order to divert resources according to the dictates of necessity and reorder his priorities according to the public good at the moment of need rather than according to the blueprint of a planned future. With limited resources of time and political support available for Presidential planning the real issue becomes not one of how to achieve an objective, but which objective deserves to be achieved and how much in the way of resources can be committed to a specific goal. However, full information is rarely at hand when Presidential action is demanded. Stephen Hess goes to the heart of the matter in his essay in stating the President should not attempt to serve as the Chief Manager of the Federal government. Hess suggests that the President is actually "Chief Political Officer of the United States. His major responsibility, in my judgement, is to make a relatively small number of highly significant political decisions each year, such as setting national priorities, which he does through the budget and his legislative proposals, and devising policy to insure the security of the country, with special attention to those situations that could involve the nation in war." Herbert Hoover, a superb administrator as President exemplifies the Chief Executive who could not grasp the political realities of his term in office or exercise the political leadership needed to rally a despairing people. Franklin Delano Roosevelt was in contrast able to provide political leadership that energetically moved the American people through the strains of an unprecedented economic depression.

THE CRISIS OF THE PRESIDENCY

One theme above all others rings through most of the following essays. Our institutions, particularly the Presidency, have served the nation well over time and should not be tampered with. Any institution, no matter how perfect in design, is only going to be as effective as the people who manage it. Nixon's brand of leadership may have failed but it was the checks of the Congress, the Supreme Court, and American public opinion that first contained him and then finally forced him to resign.

The Presidency remains the focal point of American government and politics, energizing the system through powers and programs available to no other elected official in our government. Yet democracy limits the opportunities for a highly centralized kind of executive authority as well as providing leeway for Presidents to range broadly if they can lead strongly with the support and consent of the people. Experience with our last four Presidents has taught us to lower our expectations and temper our aspirations with a healthy skepticism toward the ideas flowing from Washington. Hubert Humphrey summed up much of what has been written in these chapters when he recognized that, "The people are not necessarily asking for something new and revolutionary. They are seeking a return to fundamentals, to standards that are basic and even old fashioned. People want honesty and integrity in public life. They want decency and fair play. They want to be trusted so that they can trust their government. They are seeking character and substance, rather than charisma and image." These qualities if not definitive for the Presidency at least represent a response to presently felt needs of the American people. There is little doubt that the

American Presidency generates the thrust of our political system; the irony is that our democratic form of government remains exposed to danger whether the President has either too much or too little power.

2

A Perspective on the Presidency

George E. Reedy

Our political society is in a state of disarray. The basic signposts by which people conduct themselves have been breaking down in recent years and traditional beliefs are disintegrating. Without a more solid sense of national community we cannot expect stronger leadership to emerge.

It is not too hard to assess the state of the Presidency at this particular period in our history. Of course, it depends on a certain type of definition but I personally do not think the Presidency is any different than it has ever been. It is an office that was set forth in our federal Constitution. It is an essential office. It is one without which our government could not work, not unless we made some terribly drastic changes in the entire structure, but nevertheless it is very obvious that something has changed. And that when we talk to people today about the Office or at least about the men fulfilling it there is a certain type of indifference. Not to the Office, but to the struggle that is being made to occupy it. And to me, this is a matter of very deep concern.

If we are going to discuss the presidency today, we can discuss it the way we have here, as people with certain intellectual interests, people that engage in informed conversation on whether this should be done or that should be done to the Office. There are obviously some things wrong with it, and there are obviously structural changes that could or should be made, but of course it is not at meetings like this that the basic decisions are going to be made. It is out among the voters themselves. And no one needs to take a poll. No one needs to hire either Mr. Field or Mr. Gallup, much as I respect those two men, much as I think that they have developed their art to a very high state, to discover one very astounding thing. And that is in terms of the American people and the American voters, they could not care less. If any of you are interested in conversation stoppers, I would suggest that you walk into any gathering of American citizens that is not an intellectual gathering specifically dedicated to the Presidency, and say, Who are you supporting this year? Or who do you think is going to be President? Or who do you think should be President? You may get a couple of grunts. You are certainly going to get some blank stares and in a matter of seconds or minutes the conversation gets back on something that does interest people such as the price of ketchup, how many pickles Heinz is putting in a bottle, how the Milwaukee Brewers baseball team is making out, and what has happened to Bart Starr and the Green Bay Packers.

Now this is an important development, because it is happening at a period in our history when by all the rules, by all previous conduct, the political atmosphere should be superheated. It should be highly charged at this point, because we are living in an era that has many problems of the type which for the last 40 years we have been referring to Washington. The morning paper gave the percentage of unemployment in the United States as something like 8.3 percent. As a close reader of the *London Times,* I see that England, which has about 6 percent, is on the verge of social turmoil. The politicians are out in the street trying to explain and trying to say what they are going to do. Here we are with a much higher percentage of unemployment but you never find anyone particulalrly excited about it; I do not see anybody out in the streets picketing. No one is tearing up the paving bricks and mounting the barricades. If anything, people

seem to be somewhat complacent about it. Here we are living in
a period of very high inflation, that is high by American
standards, not high for someone who has spent some time in
Argentina, Chile, Vietnam or places like that, but that is not
what we really compare ourselves to. We compare ourselves to
past history, and by American standards we have had a very high
inflation. We are obviously surrounded by international troubles
from every point, of the compass, whether it is the Middle East
or Angola, or whether it is to the south, the north, or the west.
You would think that in a case like that, in this particular instant
of history, the thing that would be on everyone's mind is what
can we do to get a leader in the government who can resolve
these problems. And yet I will wager that even in an audience of
a Symposium on the American Presidency like this one, which is
considerably more sophisticated than the average gathering of
American citizens, that I will be very fortunate if I can find more
than four or five people who can name all of the declared
candidates. I imagine Grant Dillman, Vice President of UPI, can
do it because anybody on a wire service has to keep a list on his
desk, but maybe he cannot do it if he is away from the list. But
even more important, what I cannot find is somebody that thinks
it makes any difference.

This to me is the key, the fact that we have so many people
who do not think it makes any difference. It is very simple, but I
think overly simplistic to blame this on what has been happening
over the last 10 years, to say that the people are turned off
because of Vietnam and Watergate, that we have had so much
lying and so much chicanery in government that you have this
widespread disillusionment. And of course there is no way in the
world of proving that is not the case, but somehow I doubt it
because it does not fit our past history and it really does not fit
most of the observations that any of us can make casually about
human nature.

This is not the first time in the country that we have had
thieves in politics. There is an old story about the President's
wife who woke him up one night and said, "Darling I'm afraid
there are thieves in the house," and he said, "No darling, in the

Senate, turn over and go to sleep.'' This is not the first time in history that we have had people who have reached out for a tremendous amount of power, nor is it the first time in our history that we have engaged in some disastrous enterprises and yet we seemed to recover from those things, normally, with a very rapid recuperation after all.

Teapot Dome, which was our greatest scandal until Watergate, resulted a few months later in the election of the Vice President who had served in Office while Teapot Done was going on. The great scandals of the last part of the nineteenth century were taken in stride. The people concluded once they had thrown the rascals out and installed a new set of rascals, that the thing was over with and they were back with the system, in fact with all of the enthusiasm they had before.

What I think is happening here is something that is far deeper than scandal and far deeper than the disastrous policies in which we have engaged and I think that this is one of the reasons why we are having so much trouble with the institution of the Presidency. I do not believe the trouble is really in the institution. There is trouble in it, do not misunderstand me. But the thing I do not believe is that the major trouble is in the institution. I think it is really within our society itself and that one of our problems is that we try to examine the Presidency, and the Congress for that matter, as though they were institutions living in a vacuum somewhere and as though they had no relationship to the society in which they operate.

THE PROCESS OF LEADERSHIP

Let us examine for a moment this whole process of leadership. That usually leads to a great deal of talk about whether leaders create followers or whether followers create leaders. I think most of that is very much beside the point. I think what really happens is that leadership is a function of an interaction between politicians who are trying to get power and trying to lead society, and constituents who are looking for leadership. When we do get leaders there is some sort of catalytic arrangement that brings the two together. And when we do not get leaders, what is really happening to us is that our society has reached a stage where it is not prepared for leaders—where it lacks the necessary cement, the necessary binding force that permits groups to coalesce and to identify with some leaders or some person who is really speaking about what is on their minds. And in this particular instance, I think that it is probably well for us to go back and take a look for a moment at how the process of American poli..cs has actually worked over the last couple of hundred years.

This is a difficult undertaking because generally speaking we have a kind of nice Nellie gentility which leads us to despise all of the real workings of a democracy and impels us for some reason to establish models bearing very little relationship to reality but which we somehow consider respectable and regard as the standard by which the society has operated. We are full of clitches that will not stand up under very much examination.

We are very fond of talking about the distinction between the statesman and the politician when the only real distinction I have ever found is that the statesman is a dead politician. We are very fond of decrying logrolling when what we really mean are the various arrangements, the various tradings back and forth that are really the only way you can accommodate yourself to the necessities of a democratic government. We are very fond of lambasting the special interest groups, these selfish pressure groups, which of course are all the pressure groups to which we do not belong; the pressure groups that we belong to are those dedicated to the public interest, the pressure groups that other people belong to are those that are dedicated to plundering the treasury. And we are very fond of the assumption that somewhere out there is something called the public interest which is over and above what the people want and that the role of government is to rise above what people want to ignore the desires of people and to sustain democracy by handling the affairs of the people whether the people want them handled that way or not. And I do not know why we kid ourselves so much about this. I think at times it may be because we are something of a frontier nation. We still remember the days when the pig was in the parlor and we do not want to be that low-class "mick" that engages in horrible ugly politics and pressure groups. And therefore in the end result I think we have built for ourselves some very peculiar models of the American political scheme.

The reality is that American politics has worked as a form of brokerage among some astute and extremely skillful political leaders capable of finding means of harmonizing and regularizing all the various pressures that played upon the government and, working out of this, some form of consensus that enables the nation to act. Let us be very careful about the word "consensus". It has become one of these pejorative words. But I do not know how else you act; either there is a consensus or a minority runs the country. Either you have a consensus, or you have a dictatorship. And this concept that you cannot have a consensus, that there is something disgraceful about it, again goes back to the feeling that somewhere there is an elite group that should be allowed to run this country and it is just too bad if people do not like it.

But the point about consensus is that those politicians were operating on the basis of basic values that were much deeper and much more important than the consensus itself. The consensus was merely a practical working method with which they got bills passed, with which they were capable of bringing the country together so the country could act. Below that there was a series of values, a series of assumptions which people accepted unhesitatingly and which enabled them to identify themselves as political groups. And the interesting thing was in all of our past history most of those things could be quantified. Most people identified themselves by what they were and by what they did. A carpenter was a carpenter and he had a certain community of interest that brought him together not only with carpenters but also with other blue-collar workers. A farmer was a farmer and he had a certain community of interest that might not bring him together with every other farmer, but at least brought him together with the type of farmers that was within his particular framework. The same thing was true of businessmen, of employers. And generally speaking these people all wanted things you could quantify.

You would have, say, the blue-collar worker who wanted his dollar minimum wage (I am just pulling the figure out of thin air right now, it does not matter what the actual figure is), the farmer might want his 80 percent of parity or 90 percent, whatever it might be, and the sheep grower might want a number of conservation projects or possibly flood control projects. From this merging of special economic interests we developed politicians who could calculate within a percentage point what was necessary to keep the blue-collar worker happy. Maybe they could not give them a dollar minimum wage but they could give them 80 cents. It might not make him ecstatic but he was willing to live in the system. Maybe they could not give the farmer 90 percent of parity but they could give him 82 percent of parity. It might not make him ecstatic, but he was willing to live within the system. The same thing was true all up and down the line. And in times of crisis there was an understanding that people would respond and would respond without question—would not ask why, they would respond because we had a society in which they had confidence. Their reactions were predictable. All of a sudden we are in a society that is not predictable. Our politicians are having a terrible time because all the rules by which they have played the game are out the window. And nobody has suggested any new set of rules.

Let us go back for a second to the quantification concept. It is really amusing when you look at the various pressure groups in our society today and think of what would have happened to a Sam Rayburn or a Lyndon Johnson or a John McCormack faced with a problem of trading off 75 percent women's lib for three dams on the Snake River. My mind boggles when I look for a second to think of what would happen. I believe this is what finally ended Wilbur Mills. How in God's good name do you equate 65 percent of an excess profits tax with 45 percent of participatory democracy? How do you put together all of these new issues that are arising, things about which people obviously feel passionately, which bring them down to asking embarrassing questions (such as why aren't there more women in leadership roles in our society and I would not be surprised if within a few weeks we have somebody who wanted to know why the grade school children were not represented). Because what is happening to us is that we are beginning to get a type of society where people no longer identify themselves on the basis of a series of economic interests.

I do not believe in the old theory of economic determinism which held that people always acted in their own economic interest; I think there is too much contrary history against that one. But I do think that to a great extent, people's thinking was conditioned not by their economic interests but by the economic milieu in which they lived. This meant their thinking was known. Mr. Field or Mr. Gallup may be essential to the modern politician when it comes to taking polls to determine what the people are thinking at any given moment. But 30 or 40 years ago, no politician had to send a pollster into Gary, Indiana, to find out how those people were going to vote. Nobody would have to go into South Milwaukee, 30 or 40 years ago, to determine how the people there would react to a minimum-wage bill or to an amendment to the Taft-Hartley Act. Those things were known because the people that you had were people that came from a certain economic base and lived within it. And consequently when we were presented with problems they had a series of touchstones which gave them the kind of emotional response that guides politics.

POLITICAL BELIEFS

The mainspring of politics is really not rational consideration. This is not a cynical view at all on my part when I say that in the political field facts are really not determining but reinforcing. What really happens to us is that our politics, our political viewpoints, are really based upon certain intuitive perceptions that we have gained from the world in which we have lived, and when we have lived in a world in which we did something for the sake of survival we were capable of forming the necessary pressure groups, or we were capable of generating the necessary loyalties that enabled us to have strong political feelings and strong political leaders. And quite possibly the word loyalty might be the key to it, because I think one of the most interesting phenomena of modern times is the very rapid manner in which loyalties are breaking down; in which we are losing the unquestioned things to which we respond.

Last night, for instance, I made the statement that patriotism is dead on the American campus. I was not just particularly thinking of the American campus; I think patriotism is dead almost anywhere you go but because we are on a campus, I said on a campus. And I got challenged immediately by someone who said, "No, I'm a student, I know these students. If our country's attacked they will go and fight, but of course they'll have to know why they're going to fight." That is not patriotism in the old fashioned sense of the word. There was a time 15 or 20 years ago when they would not have had to know, when they would have just gone out and fought. And it is interesting if you go to Princeton sometime to look at a wall where they have inscribed all of the names of Princetonians who have died in wars, clear back to the Revolution. When you get to Korea and to Vietnam, the wall becomes a blank. Why? Simply because as college students they did not have to go. But there is a sharp contrast to World War II and to World War I when it was customary for whole Princeton graduating classes to march down to the recruiters office and sign up.

And I do not want any misunderstandings, I am not trying to get into an argument as whether this is or is not a good thing. If you want to argue that out save it for some course in metaphysics or some course in ethics or what have you. That is not the point of the meeting tonight. The point that I am making is that that type of touchstone—what Paul Tillich would call an un-conditioned belief—has vanished in our society and we have not yet replaced it with anything.

By and large, we are people that I think have a certain feeling of anonymity. We do not today have the old identifications that tied us so strongly to certain elements in the society. When, for example, we discussed the question of the generation gap, the interesting thing to me is not that young people rebel against their elders, because they always have. I did, my father did, everybody did, because there is a certain point in your life that you have to get rid of the people who are smothering you. You were born; somebody gave you your name; somebody taught you to talk which means they taught you how to think. At some point you have got to make your elders go away so you can find out who you are and the easiest way to make them go away is to be a Socialist if they are Republicans or come out for pot if they are from the pre-pot era. That is not what is really happening with the generation gap. What is really happening with the generation gap is an abrupt divorce of younger people from their families. Let me give you an example that I would not use except I find that so many of my friends have had something that is very similar.

My first book was on selective service and to that book Ted Kennedy wrote an introduction. I wrote a preface in which I contrasted myself as a draftee in World War II with my father who was a volunteer soldier, a young Irish kid who ran away from home when he was 12 years old. By the time he was 15, he had lied about his age and was in the cavalry and by the time he was 16 he was a one-legged war veteran, having left the other leg down in Mexico with Pancho Villa. I described how later on he was going through a foot locker and came across a picture of himself swimming in the Rio Grande with a couple of other cavalry troopers and it turned out to be two of my mother's cousins, Tom and Frank Mulvaney, who had also run away from home when they were 12 years old, lied about their ages, and became professional soldiers.

The whole point to the story was that none of them ever regretted it. Even my dad did not regret losing his leg, he said no matter what happened to him it was better than being a poor Irish kid, running a drag line in upper Michigan at 20 degrees below zero. And for Tom and Frank Mulvaney being professional soldiers was a lot better than working in a steel mill in New Albany, Indiana. And the only point I was making is the only way you are ever going to have a genuine professional Army is if you have people who are living under such circumstances that fighting in the Army is a better way of life. In talking to my youngest son about the book, I asked him what he thought about the preface. "Oh, that'll sell the book," he said, obviously thinking of Ted Kennedy's introduction. I said "No, that's not what I mean, I mean the preface I wrote." He looked at me and he said, "Oh, you mean the part about your family," and he meant that, "your family," not his family. As far as he is concerned his mother and I are the only family he has—there is nobody before that. Those of you who are my age, check your own children and find out how far back their family goes. It does not go back any further than you. And again this is because we have entered a particular stage of society where people have literally become separated from the production process, where we are no longer involved in the whole question of survival. There was a time when children participated in the family's struggle for survival and therefore felt tied to the family. Now, for many, there is no such struggle. What most of us are doing, if we are middle class, is really looking around for something to do. And it is becoming something of a strain, because in a way we have evolved a system which does not need human beings except as consumers. We have evolved a system where there are very large numbers of people who no longer can really feel that what they are doing is making a difference in society or is having an impact upon the course of the world around them.

This is true in the business world where the most important insight that I got in a year and a half of experience was the remarkable interchangeability of corporation executives. I think of them now as parts in an erector set. You can unbolt them here and put them over there. Every year we played musical chairs, the vice president in charge of motivation would come over and become vice president in charge of sales. The vice president in charge of sales would come over and become vice president of quality control. The vice president of quality control would come over and become vice president of marketing (I never figured out the difference between marketing and sales, but then I have not had a course in business administration in school). The only thing I could see for sure that made those men essential was that they all had credit cards and if you fired any of them, it might improve the production and distribution system of the corporation, but it would put a lot of restaurant owners out of the business and a lot of waiters in the economy would have a considerable slump.

When I look at the academic world, I really become appalled at the large number of Ph.D.s that I see wandering around, going to meetings of the American Political Science Association, with those hungry eyes, just hoping they can touch the coat of some professor that has tenure at a university that is not likely to fold very quickly. When I go out to the west coast—not here, but near the aerospace industries—and get into a taxicab I often discover it is being driven by a man who three or four years ago was making a good salary in the aerospace industry and now has reached the point where he cannot get a job. We are not even using human terms about these people, it has not hit us in this country yet, but I am fascinated by the euphemism of the *London Times* about people who have been fired—you aren't fired in England anymore, you are made redundant. The first time I saw this headline in the *London Times,* "5,000 redundancies at Chrysler," I thought well, I have known about their automobiles for years, but what it meant was 5,000 workers had been fired. We are treating people more and more impersonally.

Now, of course, this is not something that is hitting our country in one fell swoop. If you look around today, you will still find large numbers of people who do have something to do—mostly carpenters, plumbers, repairmen, electricians, or something like that and they still have a series of basic touchstones in their life but the numbers are shrinking. The problem is that we are getting a larger and larger number of people who are superfluous, they really have no role to play other than as consumers. And as this is happening, it is becoming more and more difficult for our political leaders to lead because there is not the necessary interaction between them and constituencies that know what they want.

I think the major theme of our political life today is confusion. We have a series of candidates, all of whom are leading very private lives. (I've become terribly amused by all the complaints of these candidates that they are not allowed any privacy. If there is one thing our candidates for the Presidency have today, it is privacy. I do not think anybody's paying any attention to them). And yet, as men, I think they are pretty good men. Or they are at least as good as many of those that we had before in terms of their quality and experience, but the point is that we have lost that connection, that coalescence between the constituencies and leadership.

I do not think this is a thing that is going to last forever. I think what will happen to us is that we are going to have political leaders who are going to go out and try to get power. They are going to come before us; they are going to appeal for our votes; they are going to try to establish some new basic values in our society, some new touchstones; and sooner or later they will succeed. But for the time being, I think that we are in one of those troughs that occurs when a society is in a very rapid state of transition—when all of the other institutions of family, church, school have broken down and new ones have yet to rise in their place. I do not pretend to have any solutions to this problem, I think anybody who has a solution just does not understand the problem. Quite possibly achieving an understanding of it leads to a way out and I hope that while we are waiting, while we are desperately trying to reestablish once again some meaning to our social life, that we do not become too concerned and do a number of things to our political institutions that later we are going to regret.

QUESTIONS AND ANSWERS

QUESTION: You said that the connection between the people and the candidates has been lost. I would think if the connection is a sense of efficacy, I agree with you, but I'm not sure what you mean by connection.

MR. REEDY: A sense of identification. The political leader stands there and he says something and a lot of people say, "My God that's my man!"

QUESTION: You said that politics had kind of broken down because values had broken down.

MR. REEDY: No, what I said is that what has broken down are the basic guideposts by which people conduct themselves, the things in which they really believe. I think that we have entered an era where people can no longer identify themselves by what they do, that you do not have people today who can say to themselves, "I am a carpenter, I am a bricklayer, I am something."

QUESTION: If I understand you correctly, you said that we are in a trough of breakdown. I'm curious, could you give us an example of another such time?

MR. REEDY: There have been plenty of them. In some respects I find the period most analogous to be that from 1850 to 1860. How many in this room can (I'll leave out Tom Cronin and one or two others), how many in this room can name the Presidents from 1850 to 1860? My God, I've got one. As a rule, I don't get anybody. I think we had the same phenomenon then, quite possibly for the same reason, that is, very rapid social change. We were just entering the industrial age during that period and institutions were breaking down. The Whig party fell to pieces, the Democratic party, what little it had been, became more and more sectarian and everybody floundered and we came out of it with the Civil War and the rise of Abraham Lincoln but I think it was very similar to this period.

QUESTION: I wanted to ask about that very period and perhaps 1917 and 1941. Everybody seems to be going back, 30 or 40 years, back to the Depression in comparison with times today and talking about groups having specific economic interests as being a former mode of policy when of course in the 1860's young men were willing to die for an abstract they called the Union and in 1917 they thought they could perhaps make the world safe for democracy and in 1941. And then in 1968, the people were dedicated to ending a war and they were, all ages of people, united upon a goal greater than themselves, and it occurred to me that we've had previous times of confusion and change with no obvious leadership but somehow in the real times of crisis there has been that hero who embodies and speaks for what people are feeling. Is there any reason why they won't happen again?

MR. REEDY: I have a lot of faith that it will happen again but I don't think it's happening right now. I'm not trying to explain tomorrow or the next day or next year but what I'm trying to look at is why it is right now we're in this situation where we do not yet have the kind of leadership and the kind of political drive and the kind of political activity that we should be expecting. I don't think you can predict the future. I think that you can analyze what's happening at the moment and quite possibly you can get some of the truth. I think you can go ahead and try to encourage the forces that you think are heading in the right direction and discourage those that you think are heading in the wrong direction. But I am terribly skeptical of human capacity to plan the future or to plan for the future. We could go back much further if we wanted to review world history. We could go back to the collapse of the Roman Empire, the collapse of the Greek Empire, the collapse of any one of a number of civilizations. You'll find plenty of examples of this happening in history before, which is why I'm not terribly discouraged about it. We always survive. What does concern me is that during this period, we may get panicky and do some things to our institutions that we will later wish we had not done. And that I think would be very bad.

QUESTION: Would you explain how a consummate Senate Majority leader like Lyndon Johnson was unable to use his political skills effectively after the first year or two of his Presidency?

MR. REEDY: Now first of all on political skill, I've written a whole book on that subject in which I've set forth a thesis that is not based on Lyndon Johnson specifically, although he looms very large in it. The thesis is that the White House always robs a man of his political skill because it places him in a certain status where he starts doing all his own thinking. Presidents really have no peers and the American system is one that very definitely requires peers. But I think that there's something deeper than that. I think that the disastrous mistakes of Vietnam and followed by Watergate probably plunged us into a realization of what was happening to us as a society but I think the forces were there anyway. I think that the forces arose out of technology, out of the constant increases in the size of government, out of the extraordinary efforts that we have made over the past number of years to transfer all social concerns to the Federal government and away from the individual. I think that all of these things played a role and I think they are the real underlying causes—the development of a system of economics which depends upon people only for consumption. I think that this became apparent to us because of the disastrous situations in Vietnam and Watergate and those I trace to the White House and to the White House isolating Presidents from political reality and to the isolation becoming extreme as the Federal government became bigger.

3

Tensions of the American Presidency

John B. Anderson

The ebb and flow of Presidential power has now led us to a point where Congressional reassertion of authority may prove to be counterproductive to the American system of government. Essentially the Presidency is the source of moral leadership in our political society and excessive constraints imposed by the Congress as in domestic and foreign affairs produce a weakened Executive with limited opportunity for initiatives designed to preserve American interests over the long term. A disciplined Congress must be linked with reasonably restrained Presidential powers to strive for national capability to cope with the complex challenges of a technological society in a world fraught with tension and conflict.

There are many perspectives from which to view the American Presidency, each of which illuminates varying facets of this unique institution. There are the scholarly works of Corwin, Rossiter, and Kallenbach—to cite only a few of those who have studied the constitutional and historical evolution of this powerful and preeminent office. There are those who treat the office of Chief Executive in the broader context of the American political process itself, a perspective taken by commentators like Daniel Moynihan, James L. Sundquist, and George Reedy. There are the chronicles of Presidential campaigns and books on life in the White House produced by authors ranging from those of counselor rank to the upstairs maid. This is not to mention innumerable biographical works, some of genuine worth and some that are all too representative of our appetite for pop culture. To any definitive bibliography of the millions of words that have been written about the Presidency must now be added a new analytical tool, oral history. Nor can we overlook the monuments of brick and mortar that dot the American landscape, buildings designed specifically to house the papers and the artifacts of ex-Presidents.

With this treasure trove to be mined, I would like to attempt a synthesis of the historical and personal perspectives. My conclusions on the state of the office and on the demands that will be made on it in America's third century are based primarily on my personal observations and reflections on the interaction between Congress and the Presidency, particularly during the period of my own service in the Congress during the last 15 years. However, there are pitfalls that beset such an approach. Fifteen years is a very thin slice indeed of America's 200-year history. Thus, it is necessary to bring the insight and objectivity of the long view of history to bear on the attempt to evaluate the Presidency from the short-term perspective—to leaven the contemporary assessment with the lessons of history.

EVOLUTION OF PRESIDENTIAL AND CONGRESSIONAL RELATIONS

An examination of the institution of the Presidency over the past nineteen decades gives rise to an image of an amoeba, tracing its way across the face of a microscope slide, its shape constantly changing in response to stimuli, some visible and some unviewed. In my opinion, appraisals of the Presidency should be viewed in the context of a living organism. A description of contemporary Presidential prerogatives and powers, for example, is akin to examining a freeze-dried amoeba, a still photograph of an ongoing, evolving process, an institution with a life of its own—an institution that ineluctably changes from one era to the next. It is an inevitable procedure somewhat like the evolutionary process of natural selection. If America's governing institutions were born of a hide-bound constitution, and thus were rigidly constituted, no doubt they would snap at the first sign of stress. Instead, it fairly may be argued that the three branches of our government are flexible and are open to new interpretations by each succeeding generation. They are an institutional affirmation of the biological ''law'' of the survival of the fittest.

There are a number of ways that the evolution of our institutions may be charted. One perspective is to observe how the balance of power has shifted between the Congress and the President during the past two centuries. It is a useful way to assess the executive branch in any given era and to weigh its impact in the constitutional context. Not everyone agrees that the fluctuating balance of power, washing back and forth as it has between the executive and legislative branches, has been, for the most part, salutary. ''It would seem as if a very wayward fortune had presided over the history of the Constitution of the United States inasmuch as that great Federal charter has been alternately violated by its friends and defended by its enemies.'' This, the opening line of Woodrow Wilson's classic study, *Congressional Government,* was written in 1883-84.

Wilson's study, in spite of his rather rigid stop-frame view of American government, is a starting point for an account of the ebb and flow of power between the Executive and the Legislature. In his book, the President-to-be noted with a degree of alarm common to most chief executives that ''Congress is fast becoming the governing body of the nation, and yet the only power which it possesses in perfection,'' he noted incredulously, ''is the power which is but a part of government, the power of legislation.'' Wilson's view was distorted, of course, by his apparent reluctance to look at the Presidency and the Congress as a continuum. The ''power of legislation'' is considerably more potent that Wilson imagined. However, his comments in context were quite understandable because Wilson grew up in an era of weak presidents like Andrew Johnson, Grant, Hayes, Garfield, and Arthur. By 1900, while writing the preface to the 15th edition of his study, Wilson detected that power was flowing back to the Oval Office and that the President was "at the front of affairs."

As Walter Lippmann pointed out in his introduction to a 1955 edition of the Wilson book, Wilson lived through three distinct phases of the American constitutional system. The first phase was that of his youth—the third quarter of the 19th century. The second began with Grover Cleveland's Presidency in the mid-1880's and extended through the administration of Theodore Roosevelt and into Wilson's, ending in 1918. It was a period characterized by strong Presidents and by Wilson's own observation that the power of a President was almost boundless: "His office is anything he has the sagacity and force to make it." The third phase, witnessed only in part by Wilson, commenced during his second term and ended when the second Roosevelt took office in 1933. That period was characterized by weak Presidents, like Harding and Coolidge, and it signaled a renaissance of Congressional power.

Of the three eras of government observed by Wilson, perhaps the most pertinent to a study of the contemporary Presidency is the period of Congressional government lamented by Wilson.

That particular period began on a dramatic note, with Congress wresting from President Andrew Johnson control of post-Civil War reconstruction policy. During Johnson's tenure, Congress established an unprecedented hegemony over Federal policy by asserting unchallenged control over executive personnel practices (1867 Tenure of Office Act) and by impeaching and almost convicting the embattled Andrew Johnson.

Johnson's lackluster successors, beginning with Grant, were either uninterested or unable to loosen Congress's hammerlock on the government. The Tenure of Office Act, which stipulated that the Senate must approve of the firing of any Presidential appointee, gave Congress the clout it needed, and for 30 years the Senate and the House—in the absence of a civil service or merit system—meddled in the thousands of patronage appoint-ments that had traditionally been the executive's province.

Right after the Civil War, Congress also began to reassert its control over the Federal government's receipts and expenditures, a constitutional responsibility vested in an apparently dis-interested Congress.

During this period, as historian and Presidential scholar James MacGregor Burns notes, Congress also began to reassert its "basic authority to frame legislation." Although a substantial amount of the legislation was what one scholar has called "of individual application," the fact remains that during this time Congress exerted a strong degree of legislative dominance over the executive.

One of the reasons that Congress was able to wield so much power in such an impressive fashion was the fault of its constitutional opponent. The opposition was often weak. In other words, it was not only Congress's ability to ride roughshod over the executive; it was also the seeming willingness of chief executives of the time to let it happen. Too many of them were weak, indecisive, without authority. Even a politically-prominent, nationally-popular figure like General Ulysses Grant was not inclined to gather the reins of power to himself in the White House. Historian Edward S. Corwin (writing in 1940) on the subject: "Of the 33 individuals who have filled the office not more than one in three has contributed to the development of its powers; under other incumbents things have either stood still or gone backward."

Other periods of history could be examined, but let us come quickly to the present. It was in the Fall of 1973 that reporter Elizabeth Drew, a perspicacious observer of the Washington scene, filed this report as seen through Congress's eyes:

> When the 93rd Congress convened at the beginning of this year, many politicians were saying that the imbalance of power between the legislative and executive branches was such that we were facing a "constitutional crisis. . . ."

But causes for their expressions of concern were
apparent enough. The President was unilaterally termi-
nating programs and impounding money. The "carpet
bombing" of North Vietnam over the Christmas
holidays was sufficiently contrary to the growing
Congressional opposition to the war that it had been
done while the lawmakers were out of town. Several
lawmakers thought that the bombing lacked legal
authority. Major policymakers were refusing to appear
before the Congress to explain their policies. The
Attorney General, stretching the doctrine of "executive
privilege" to unprecedented breadth, stated that the
President could prevent anyone in the executive branch
from appearing before or releasing any documents to the
Congress. The President did not trouble himself to make
the traditional trip down Pennsylvania Avenue to deliver
a State of the Union message, but instead sent it to the
Capitol by messenger.

Little more than two years has passed, yet the scene has
again shifted dramatically. A resurgent Congress has restricted
Presidential impoundments, the Supreme Court in a unanimous
decision has made it perfectly clear that there are limits to the
doctrine of executive privilege. Among other actions, the
Congress has with respect to Southeast Asia, the Sinai
Agreement and most recently and very much in the news today,
Angola, intervened massively in the President's conduct of
external affairs. We are, in so many words, on the verge of
another era of "congressional government," and the chief
instrument of the renaissance resembles its predecessor: "the
power to legislate."

It is a power to be reckoned with. One student of the
legislative process, examining the period from 1890-1940,
determined that of the 90 major pieces of legislation enacted
during that time, the President could be given credit for
approximately 20% of the bills. Congress, on the other hand,
was credited with responsibility for about 40 percent of the total
(30 percent were the result of Congressional and Presidential

cooperation or interaction, and less than 10 percent were credited to "external" pressure groups). Another study indicates the executive and the legislature share about the same ratios of responsibility for major legislation since World War II.

This rather quantative analysis is only a partial indicator of what is happening. What we have witnessed for the past two years is a sleeping giant come awake, stretching its muscles, building them anew. Congress has, I believe, begun to reassert its proper constitutional role. There are those who would label the Congressional resurgence an "encroachment" on Presidential prerogatives. In a sense it is, for Congress is attempting to exercise more control over the Federal government than it did during the first three-fourths of this century. Recent actions by Congress have had a very discernible impact on how the Presidency functions in this country today, so it is worthwhile to review some of them.

REASSERTION OF CONGRESSIONAL AUTHORITY

Impoundment Control

In spite of the very clearly stated dictum in the Federalist Papers that "the legislative department alone has access to the pockets of the people . . .," for so many years Congressional control of the pursestrings was limited to the appropriations process. (The reason is simple: who ever heard of a taxpayers' revolt against unauthorized or excessive expenditures? The most recent one on record, according to an English historian, occurred in 1469!) But by 1974, there was no need of a taxpayers' revolution to galvanize the Congress and goad it into action. The issue: impoundment.

Ever since the time of Jefferson, U.S. Presidents had refused to spend money that had been authorized to fund programs created by Congress. The practice, which amounts in the words of one contemporary U.S. Senator to an "informal line-item veto," was in general restricted to military matters and foreign affairs. And in the nineteenth century, impoundment was practiced on a relatively small scale. In this century, up until Richard Nixon's time, impoundment has been used primarily as a method of reducing unnecessary or wasteful military expenditures. Franklin Roosevelt, Truman, Eisenhower, Kennedy, and Johnson all used their impoundment power in relatively restrained ways.

President Nixon, though, embroidered on the executive's traditional use of impoundment, and began holding back the expenditure of Federal funds for domestic programs. By 1971, toward the end of Nixon's first term in office, there were estimates that his administration had impounded between $12 billion and $25 billion in funds appropriated and authorized by Congress for Federal programs. By 1972-73 large cuts, not authorized by Congress, were being made in agriculture (Rural Environmental Assistance Program, Water Bank Program, MHA's emergency disaster loan program, rural electricity action program, water and sewer grants), environment (waste treatment funds were halved), and housing (18-month moratorium on subsidized housing programs, holdbacks on community development funds).

In 1974 in response to the chief executive's escalated use of the impoundment technique, Congress passed the Budget and Impoundment Control Act (P.L. 93-344), a law that places severe restrictions on the President's ability to hold back expenditures of money for Federal programs created by Congress. In effect, the President can no longer refuse (except for a limited time) to spend appropriated funds unless Congress gives its approval, nor can he indefinitely postpone such spending if Congress disapproves it. If the President decides that certain appropriations are not required and should be rescinded or reserved from obligation, he must transmit a special message requesting a rescission of the budget authority; unless both Houses pass a rescission bill within 45 days, the budget appropriation must be made available for obligation. If the President sends a message to Congress recommending the deferral, withholding or delaying of the availability of any funds for obligation, the President must obligate those funds if either House passes an impoundment resolution disapproving the proposed deferral (no time limit).

Resolutions disapproving Presidentially-proposed deferrals of expenditures were passed by the Senate in 1975 which in effect ordered spending of funds for biomedical and environmental research, nuclear materials, laser fusion, thermonuclear research, comprehensive planning grants, Federal-aid highway funds, Youth Conservation Corps, Columbia Basin Irrigation project, emergency energy conservation services program, and a fruit crop laboratory.

Congress disapproved in 1975 a number of sizable rescissions proposed by the President in appropriations made for the Departments of HEW, HUD, Commerce, and Air Force and for the FBI, Forest Service, IRS, and the Hill-Burton hospital construction program.

Legislative Veto

Just as Congress has acquired a heretofore unrealized measure of control over Federal spending, by exerting control of the chief executive's "line-item veto," so too has it turned increasingly to another law maker's tool, the legislative veto. The word "increasingly" may not do justice to the tremendous upswing in the use of this device, which has been in use since 1932. Since that time, the legislative veto has been employed approximately 180 times—an average of about four vetoes per year. But this yearly average is misleading, for during the first half of the 1932-1975 time period, there was an average of only about one veto per year by Congress. Here is the breakdown:

1932-1939	5 legislative vetoes	
1940-1949	15	''
1950-1959	35	''
1960-1969	46	''
1970-1975	80	''

In fact, the pace is quickening. In the first session of the 94th

Congress alone, at least 23 legislative vetoes were passed by Congress.

There are three basic elements of the legislative veto: (1) Congress stipulates that particular executive decisions must be submitted to Congress (or to its committees), thus deferring implementation, for a prescribed waiting period (commonly 30-60 days, but the range has been as much as 5 days to 3 years); (2) Congress reserves the right to disapprove of the proposed executive action, by taking action itself on the Floor or in Committee within the time span allotted by Congress; and (3) Congress limits its action to an "up or down" action on the proposal.

While only a few statutes that Congress has passed place an actual limit on Presidential powers directly, many of them restrict the activities of executive departments and agencies that are part of the executive branch. There can be no doubt that Congress is exercising hereby some rather strong restrictions on Presidential power and prerogatives.

OTHER CONGRESSIONAL POWERS

There is a host of other active powers available to the Congress by virtue of its power to legislate, and in recent years they have been used increasingly to stake out limits—some broadly defined, others more narrow in scope—to Presidential power.

Appropriations

In the 93rd and 94th Congresses, stipulations were added to at least 12 different appropriations bills, restricting such executive branch activities as prohibiting expenditures of funds to support U.S. combat activities in Southeast Asia after August 15, 1973; prohibiting military assistance to Turkey during the Cyprus crisis; prohibiting use of Federal funds to finance forced busing of school children; and others.

Military and Defense

The 93rd Congress passed the War Powers Resolution requiring the President to consult with Congress before sending U.S. forces into hostile areas. The President is directed to report to Congress within 48 hours on any such action, setting forth his constitutional and legislative authority and estimating the scope and duration of U.S. involvement. He must terminate U.S. intervention within 60 days unless Congress declares war, extends the period of another 60 days, or specifically authorizes the use of force.

In addition to other measures, the Congress also passed a prohibition of increasing the total number of U.S. tactical nuclear warheads in Europe except in the case of actual hostilities.

Foreign Affairs

In the past three years, Congress has also invaded the President's traditional sanctum, foreign policy, by imposing no fewer than nine separate restrictions on how the Chief Executive may do business with other nations. Items include requirements that military base agreements be submitted to Congress, advance notice be given of the President's intention to sell defense articles or services, certain types of trade agreements, security arrangements in the Sinai, and agricultural commodities agreements and understandings.

These are just some of the ways that the Congress has brought pressure to bear on Presidential power and prerogatives in the past three years. The President, on the other hand, is not without his own resources, constitutional or otherwise. In the past 75 years, for example, the White House staff has increased over five-hundred-fold: by 1973, the President employed 510 people on his *personal* staff. By then, the Executive Office of the President, which includes not only his personal staff, the Domestic Council, and almost two dozen other offices, advisory councils, and special projects staffs (such as Telecommunications Policy, Science and Technology, Consumer Affairs, Council of Economic Advisors), employed over 2,200 people at an annual cost of $41 million. The contrasts with the turn-of-the-century White House are impressive but more recent comparisons are more revealing: in 1955, the White House's annual bill was slightly less than $10 million. In only twenty years, it has grown fourfold. At the same time, the number of permanent White House positions has grown from 1400 to 2200. A 1973 report of the growth of the Executive Office of the President put it another way: in 1955 there was one White House executive-level employee ($30,000 or more per year) for every 1,920 Federal employees. By 1972, there was one White House executive for every 403 Federal employees.

Despite the burgeoning of resources of the executive branch, the recent assertion of power by Congress raises the question: is the balance of power—for so long admittedly in favor of the Chief Executive—shifting toward Congress? Or does the Congress' renaissance signal only a modest shift, a redress of an imbalance that will result in two more equal partners? Taken in the context of the continuum—the ongoing ebb and flow of power among the three branches of government—the question cannot be answered with any reasonable degree of finality. That the question must be asked, however, is an abiding concern of mine.

Norman C. Thomas, in the introduction to his recently-edited book, *The Presidency in Contemporary Context,* writes that Congressional-Presidential conflict has always been latent in the American constitutional system, but only since 1965 has such conflict become a permanent feature of national politics. His conclusion is that constitutional conflict now exceeds the bounds that produce merely a creative tension and has assumed the proportion of a malfunction in the democratic process. To wit, the most recent session of Congress which ended on a note of extreme bitterness over the basic question of fiscal policy. Who has the right to set a spending ceiling? Congress with its basic constitutional power to appropriate and raise revenues—and equipped now with its new procedures under the Budget Control and Anti-Impoundment Act, or the President? Congress can make a plausible consititutional and statutory case. Yet it is the President who has not only the statutory authority but the responsibility to submit annually the budget of the United States government. Federal fiscal policy has become an essential component of any formula designed to produce stable economic growth. Keynesians, neo-Keynesians, or non-Keynesians should be able to agree on that simple proposition. The authors of the Budget Control Act specifically claimed that it was conceived for the purpose of producing a Congressional budget despite such accoutrements as a Congressional Budget Office and semi-annual Congressional budget resolutions.

As the title of the new law implies, it was designed to be a budget *control* mechanism. However, in a proclaimed era of Congressional government the institution is no longer to merely dispose of what a President proposes, particularly when that President is a member of the opposite political party and is running for election to an office he now holds by appointment. If a President is going to be held responsible for the prosperity of the nation, how can we distribute this authority over federal fiscal policy to make the degree of accountability clear to the American people?

Richard Nixon used to be fond of quoting Winston Churchill's phrase "to govern is to choose." Rhetorically we may ask, How can a President possibly administer the fiscal policy of the nation when he is not given the opportunity to choose between what he regards as a stimulative or a contractionary budget? This, in turn, suggests that the politics of confrontation could be replaced by the politics of consensus and conciliation if the American people would simply elect a President and a Congress of the same party. The polls, however have recently suggested that divided government may not be merely a temporary phenomenon, and that the voters discern some good in a division of responsibility between the two branches along party lines.

The argument can be made that it is enough to leave the people as ultimate arbiters of who is right or wrong on the spending issue in biennial congressional elections or every four years when we elect a President. However, prolonged confrontation on important economic issues can have an adverse impact on the general welfare because of the lack of confidence that it engenders among producers, consumers, and investors alike.

Therefore, I believe it will be necessary to come to a resolution of the current impasse that will require more than the temporary accommodation between the President and the Congress reached in December when elliptical phrases papered over a fundamental disagreement on fiscal philosophy.

I have come to the conclusion that given its new resources provided under the Budget Control Act, Congress could propose a budget which it would attempt to reconcile with the Executive branch budget submission through its House and Senate budget committees sometime before the fiscal year begins. This would discipline the Congress to the necessity of offering more than negative strictures with respect to the Presidential budget. If differences remained, the Congress would pass its version of the federal budget, but permit the President the exercise of an item veto. The Illinois Constitution of 1970 provided for an item veto on appropriation bills, plus the power to make amendatory changes in other legislation as well. In both instances, a majority of the members elected to each house would be required to restore the reduced appropriation to its original amount or to accept the amendatory changes in other legislation. Obviously, a change in Article I, Section 6 of the U.S. Constitution would be required to follow the Illinois example. The difficulties inherent in such a suggestion are recognized. However, I wonder if a clearer definition of ultimate responsibility for decisions on fiscal matters and a sharing of that responsibility would not produce far more comity between the branches than now exists. It could deter omnibus appropriation bills for fear of an exercise of the item veto and correspondingly produce an impetus for multi-year authorizations and appropriations.

FOREIGN AFFAIRS AND NATIONAL SECURITY

Any discussion of Presidential leadership must deal with the sensitive area of foreign affairs and national security. Regretfully, it is another area where the concept of "creative tension" has run amok. In the concluding chapter to his excellent book, *A Responsible Congress: The Politics of National Security,* Alton Frye maintains that a stronger Congress does not mean a weaker President. Yet, Congress and the President are not cooperating in the sensitive area of foreign policy. The obvious problem is to clear away the rubble of suspicion and distrust of executive action that is our Viet Nam legacy. Unfortunately, the atmospherics of an election year do not provide the most auspicious climate to begin anew. The mounting drum fire of criticism of the policy of detente, compounded now by such Soviet actions as a more repressive immigration policy, involvement in Angola (along with the evidence of our own intervention), pose a serious threat to the goal of reestablishing a bipartisan foreign policy. There can be no question of the necessity for not only consultation but a sharing of a responsibility between the President and the Congress for ultimate decisions that involve war or peace.

Part of the problem, however, is a failure on the part of Presidents alone to articulate clearly what U.S. policy is. And the advent of the State of the World message did not really help to solve that problem. The smog of generalities that we have heard about building a structure of peace really served only to obscure, rather than to illuminate such basic questions as: What are our basic American interests? What are the legitimate limits to the use and the exercise of American power?

If there is an undisputed area for moral leadership by a President it is this area of America's role in world affairs. At a recent meeting of the Tri-Lateral Commission, Columbia University Professor Zbigniew Brzezinski observed that the great passion of the last two centuries was the desire for freedom. The battle cry of the developing countries of the world for the coming age has been transformed to a demand for equality. He went on to suggest that the line of conflict is no longer as much between East and West as it is between North and South. For it is in the countries of the Southern hemisphere that seeds of conflict will be nourished unless the countries of the industrialized and developed North perceive this new and emerging challenge to a stable world order. The President of the world's most powerful and affluent democracy is confronted with the awesome task of communicating a new vision of our altered global responsibilities.

Especially in foreign affairs, the well-recognized doctrine of judicial restraint should help govern our actions. The Supreme Court has generally sought to avoid the application of its power in a manner which would put it on a collision course with either the Executive or Legislative branches. There have been exceptions from the time of *Marbury v. Madison* to the recent decision involving the claim of executive privilege in the case of the Watergate tapes. But the general principle is firmly anchored in constitutional law. As a general rule, in my view, Congress has a similar obligation to refrain from actions which provoke an ultimate confrontation in matters involving national security and foreign policy. This past session of Congress has been one that has been marred by some instances where both House and Senate failed, in my judgment at least, to observe that salutory principle. The most notable example is the embargo on military assistance to Turkey, one of our NATO allies.

Another example is the action Congress took in adopting the Jackson-Vanick amendment denying most-favored-nation treatment to the Soviet Union. It is an example of Congressional action which although clearly within the Constitutional prerogatives of the Legislative Branch was an unwise and counterproductive exercise of power. One of the most disabling features of these periodic Congressional forays into foreign policy has been the tendency to subordinate—if not to subvert—long term policy goals to the exigencies of short term political advantage. The requirements of continuity and certitude for foreign policy are sacrificed for the passing tides of public passion on a given issue. In this connection I would cite the effort to use the State Department Appropriations Bill as a vehicle to influence the course of delicate negotiations with the Republic of Panama for a new treaty dealing with U.S.

sovereignty in the Canal Zone. To ward off this kind of unwise intervention by the Legislaltive Branch, the Chief Executive must adequately discharge his responsibilities of articulating what the goals of his administration really are and he must do that not simply in the sense of going over the heads of the Congress to the people, for consultation on a timely and continuous basis can reduce the necessity for that tactic.

In spite of the clarity afforded by the multifarious perspectives on the Presidency, it is not easy to develop a picture of the institution in sharp focus. In short, we now "see through a glass darkly," to adopt the age-old wisdom of St. Paul. To cite a more contemporary reference, Theodore Sorensen in his book of last year, *Watchman on the Walls,* confesses that it was only somewhat later in his service to President Kennedy that he realized that he viewed 'the office of the Presidency merely as the reflected image of Kennedy himself—rather than with the detachment that comes from an understanding that the institution is far more than the lengthened shadow of the temporary occupant of the Oval Office.

A few examples will suffice to show how this overly personalized approach to the Presidency can be so destructive.

It was Franklin Roosevelt who gave us the phrase that the Presidency must be pre-eminently a position of moral leadership. In both domestic and foreign affairs he proceeded in the judgment of most people to redeem that pledge. There is abundant evidence that he could be petty, bureaucratic, vindictive, willful, and even resentful of the constitutional restraints imposed upon him by a constitutional system based on a separation of powers. Yet, on the larger slate of history, he wrote a record of remarkable accomplishment. His administration saw the origins of the modern Presidency. The Roosevelt era demonstrated the capacity of the Presidential office to provide moral leadership for America. Today, because of recent revelations of illegal surveillance and domestic spying by the FBI, and an abuse of power by the CIA that stretches back over the course of at least the last four administrations, not to mention the incubus of Watergate that still haunts our national conciousness, the person who mentions moral leadership in conjunction with the Presidency is likely to be greeted by scorn.

Yet I believe that the words that the late Walter Lippmann wrote in 1932 when we were still descending the Gadarene slope of another national crisis are as timely now as when they were written. Of the American people he wrote:

> They are looking for leaders, for men who are truthful and eloquent and resolute in the conviction that the American destiny is to be free and to be magnanimous. They are looking for leaders who will talk to the people about their duty and about the sacrifices that they must impose upon themselves and about their responsibility to the world and to posterity, about all things that make a people self-respecting and serene and confident. May they not look in vain.

That, I believe, is as good a definition of moral leadership that we Americans will find. But the skeptic will rightfully reply that the people may not follow the beacon of presidential moral leadership. Maybe some of the hubris has gone out of our feelings about this high office, but James McGregor Burns in his book on Presidential government, *The Crucible of Leadership*, says this, "In Presidential government Americans have established one of the most powerful political institutions in the free world. They have fashioned sometimes unwittingly a weapon that has served them well in the long struggle for freedom and equality at home and in the search for stable and democratic policies abroad. They have grasped the uses of this power, and as Harold Laski has said, 'great power makes great leadership possible.' Yet power alone is inadequate, it must be linked with purpose."

And so I hope that with discipline and self-imposed restraint, we in the Legislative Branch will not seek to supplant an imperial Presidency with an imperial Congress. Let us instead link power with purpose and let that purpose be not simply to strive for an aggrandizement of institutional power but for the broader goal of a more just and humane society for all the American people.

COMMENTARIES AND RESPONSE

GEORGE E. REEDY: What I am going to do is throw out several thoughts that take off from what Congressman Anderson had to say. I think I'm going to begin with his closing, because he brings out a point where I have a considerable amount of disagreement. And what I'm trying to do is not to provoke an argument so much as to place a certain perspective upon the subject matter and upon these essays. I, myself, think that political analysis, political science, is very closely allied to philosophy because it represents a search for reality. And I'm not certain that most of the conferences that we attend on the Presidency or on the American system of government really got very close to reality. I think to a certain extent we have a tendency to build models, the plaything of the behavioral sciences and in the building of our models we assume that if we attain a certain amount of symmetry, if we're capable of building our model in such a way that it doesn't explode in our faces, we have somehow arrived at the truth. And I think at times we get into a form of circular reasoning. One of these is whether the Congress is going to supplant the Presidency or whether the President is going to supplant the Congress.

The point I'd like to make there is I think that that's not only a totally irrelevant consideration, but that it has no relationship to reality whatsoever. What you have are competing bodies, but competing in the sense of possibly competing for national attention, which the Founding Fathers set up to do two different things. And neither one is going to do the job that is done or should be done by the other and that so-called Congressional government does not mean a Congressional government at all; it merely means the Executive is not doing his job and the so-called Presidential government merely means that Congress is not doing its job. I'd like to put it this way, I think the purpose of Congress is to secure consent and what that really means is to arrive at political understanding and that means there is a certain limitation upon what Congress can do. I think where I disagree the most strongly with Congressman Anderson is over the word that everybody loves, a "responsible" Congress. I've been looking at that word responsible for years and the only definition that I can give you of responsible is any point of view that agrees with mine. And the only definition I can give you of irresponsible is any point of view that disagrees with mine. And when you have a purely political body what it means is that if that body does not have constituencies that have some form of agreement, some form of consensus, it's rather idle to talk about responsibility.

You are not going to have agreement in our political institutions unless there is agreement within the United States. And I think what has happened to us is that for a long period of time, we have had Presidents who have been governing without political consent. Not necessarily because we had Presidents who were overreaching themselves, many a politician will overreach himself if given the opportunity, but certainly because the basic fundamental qualities that lead to consent and consensus are not there. And one of the reasons that we have gotten into so much trouble is that Presidents, the Executive Branch of the government, which is there primarily to exercise the power of the people and to carry out the day-to-day attitude of the government have been confronted with a number of problems for which they could not really secure a consensus. That is one of the big problems with Vietnam; it was a policy that I disagreed with, that I thought was badly wrong, but I think the real mischief of it was not that it was wrong but that we were put into it without first securing consent. Almost any politician sooner or later is going to get into a disastrous set of circumstances; human beings are not infallible, human beings are not perfect. Consequently most administrations sooner or later are going to stumble into disastrous consequences. If they first secured consent, however, I do not believe those mistakes are going to tear the country to pieces.

Now the second point that I wish to make is very closely allied to this. It is in a sense that we're here to talk about the Presidency, we're not really talking about the Presidency, that is, we're not if we're going to get anywhere near reality. But what we have to talk about is our society itself. There are some problems connected with the Office but fundamentally the problem is one of our society itself in which we do not have the broad type of consensus which enables a government to act and to act with some decisiveness. We keep talking about the Presidency as being the focal point of our national life. I think that's true. But usually we make the statement and then don't think there are really implications but the implications are rather sharp. What it really means is that when we speak of the United States as acting, what we mean is the President is acting. If the United States acts in a foreign crisis of some sort, what it means is that the President sends troops somewhere, or the President promises somebody some dough, or the President promises somebody that he won't give him some dough, or the President orders that Central Intelligence Agency to do something. The reality is that as a nation we act through the President. And I think we are in one of those periods in history where we as a people are in a strange period of transition in which there is no possibility for the moment of getting the kind of consensus that is going to give Presidents the authoritative ability to act. I don't think it is a question of having weak Presidents and weak political leaders.

I think it's a question that we ourselves, our society, have not succeeded at this point in adjusting to the new circumstances of our world. If anything, I believe that this is a period that bears a very strong resemblance historically to the decade from 1850 to 1860 or quite possibly the decade from 1920 to 1932 when our country was undergoing some profound social and economic changes. And at the moment, I don't think that we are going to get at our problems, I'm against the item veto for instance, but I don't propose to make an argument out of it because I don't think it's that important. I think the important issue before us as a people is to try to reestablish our sense of community, to try to reestablish our sense of values, and to try one again to get the type of consensus upon which Presidents can act.

GERALD WARREN: The order of these commentaries on Congressman Anderson's paper gives me a chance to speak in somewhat rebuttal to George Reedy. While I agree with his conclusion, his hypothesis leading up to it lost me a little bit. I agree that we do need a consensus, I disagree that we will ever have complete consensus and I think the crucial thing that Mr. Reedy and Mr. Anderson said was that we want our leaders to lead, we want them to shape events, and to focus a symposium such as this on the Presidency, I think loses sight of what is really necessary and that is to demand excellence in our leaders in Congress, in city councils, state legislatures, on school boards, all across this country, in the universities across this country, in churches, in newspapers. I really think that is what is necessary. The expectations that we place on the Presidency of the United States seem to be extreme and unnatural. I think that we are going through a period of time where we should devote as much time as possible on what we should expect of the Congress. I think if the Congress wants to and can exert its influence on foreign policy it should make very clear what its rules are and adhere to them as it did not do in the Angola situation, and perhaps the impression is not so much that the leadership of the Executive is in question but the leadership of the Congress is and does that need restructuring, and will ever again a Congress, a Senate, a House of Representatives believe its leaders.

It seems to me if we are to gain any sort of consensus as George Reedy speaks of, we must be sure that means our leaders at all levels of the community and of the nation are truly representative of us.

JOHN B. ANDERSON: George Reedy very kindly said he didn't want to pick an argument with me and I have not taken offense at George in any sense of the word with what he has had to say, except that I question what seems to me a fundamental premise of his statement and that is that what we need is a consensus, the only thing that's going to produce forward movement in the country is consensus. As I look back on a whole array of actions that were taken under Lyndon Johnson, who of course made consensus government famous with the slogan, "come let us reason together," and so we had a consensus, fine. We passed a whole series of bills, everything from highway beautification, you name it. It all happened in the fabulous 89th Congress and it seems to me that much of the alienation of the country, much of the disenchantment with big government, much of the cynicism on the part of people with government which promises very much and produces very little is that apparently that consensus broke down and the programs were not executed at least in such fashion that we retained the confidence of the people who produced that consensus. So I would question whether or not a President can recline on a bed of ease and assume that consensus is going to solve the problems. I think that occasionally a President has to take a pretty lonely position on a certain issue if he is going to really lead, in the finest, truest sense of the definition of that term "leadership" and I still believe that is the outstanding attribute that any successful President must have—he must be able to lead. That sometimes requires taking positions which do not represent a consensus within the country, but somehow he must inspire the kind of moral vision that the people should have lest they perish.

4

Public Opinion and Presidential Response

Mervin D. Field

It is fallacious to assume that voters separate themselves into blocs and that they respond to issues in a united and predictable way. Qualities that voters most look for in a Presidential candidate include honesty and trustworthiness with less emphasis on experience, leadership ability, intelligence and education. Voters are most negative about qualities of dishonesty and deceitfulness in a candidate.

American public opinion and the public attitude toward the Presidency is made up of an incredible variety of components. No matter how insightful the legion of political scientists, researchers, political reporters are, and despite the large body of attitudinal data derived from surveys, it is still an impossible task to correctly interpret how the public feels.

As a consequence, I am relieved that these essays span such a broad spectrum of issues concerning the Presidency and that more that a score of illustrious participants from a variety of disciplines and experiences are offering their perspectives. In the space allotted to me, I would like to discuss a number of elements related to public opinion and the Presidency.

1. The fallacy of assuming that voters separate themselves into blocs and that they respond to issues in a unified and predictable

way. The so-called "youth vote" is a good example of one pitfall in this kind of thinking.

2. Some of the qualities the public has indicated that it desires in Presidential candidates.

3. Some implications of the public's disenchantment with the Office of the President and other institutions that surveys have found to exist.

4. Some speculations about what I think may be the consequences of increasing information on the public's view of the Presidency.

5. A defense of the present primary system which is a current target of reformers of our political system.

It is most useful to see American public opinion as being made up of differing views held by a number of different segments rather than seeing it as a mass public.

Simply stated, segmentation theory argues that there is an audience of some size for any kind of message, or a market of some size for any kind of product, and there are separate markets for each variation of that message or product. This theory has recently found wide application in marketing, but it is not a new idea. Successful political leaders in democratic societies for centuries have based their strategies on the idea of segmentation. They have always known that there were blocs of voters out there with widely different interests, hopes, and fears which require separate appeals, treatments, or actions. This has been the operating policy of good politicians since at least ancient Greece.

Politicians of the modern era nevertheless seem to have been seduced by "mass media" into behaving as though there were a "mass electorate". However, the rise of systematic public opinion research, with its computer apparatus allowing one to compare quickly opinions and attitudes across a host of population subgroups, has given the segmentation concept new life. It is a powerful tool and analysis of these data is leading to some new conceptions about political behavior.

MYTH OF THE YOUTH VOTE

One of the cautions I would like to leave with you today is that this practice of trying to understand our society better by breaking down the whole into its smaller parts, can easily mislead us into new fallacies. A lot of what we think we know may not be so on closer examination.

I'll illustrate this with examples of data on one of these segments often sorted out for special attention or analysis— youth, young adults, young voters.

I have observed over the years vast differences in behavior, voting preferences, and perceptions of the political process *within* this narrowly defined age segment of 18 to 24 year-olds which represent about 9 percent of the total population and about 19 percent of the population 18 and over. Significant differences often are found between those 18 to 20 year-olds and those 21-24 year-olds. There are often wholesale differences in perceptions and political behavior between young men and young women within this age bracket. Further, there is usually wide variability between those who are having or have had college experience and those who have not. Within the group with college experience, wide differences of opinion on political issues are seen between engineers and English majors, between chemists and psychologists, between MBA's and Ph.D's, and so on. There is wide variability between the young person depending on whether he or she is married, white, Black, Latino, working or not, and if working the kind of job held.

This illustrates how the broad brush that so many of us tend to apply when we want to describe a group or bloc of voters may conceal more than it reveals even when we sort out what is believed to be a homogeneous segment such as "younger voters." It is necessary to use second and third order analysis and beyond to get at the true segment boundaries that make a difference. And the further we have to fragment a bloc of voters to find a difference, the smaller the fragments become, and thereby obviate the merit of doing the analysis in the first place.

Four years ago strategists for Senator George McGovern early in the Presidential campaign saw the youth of this country as a homogeneous bloc of voters which could win the election for him. McGovern because of his stand on Vietnam and other issues projected a strong appeal to the youth of this country. Initially when McGovern was showing up in the preference polls with just 5 percentage points, three or four of these points came from younger voters.

McGovern's aides had as their goal to register 15 million of the 23 million adults between the ages of 18 to 24, and they projected that Senator McGovern could gain a plurality of 10 million votes in just this age group alone. This harvest of the anticipated "youth vote" would offset any vote deficits in other groups and would provide the margin for victory.

As you know, there were a number of failures in implementing this fond dream. First, there was the difficulty of reversing the normal behavior of young people which consistently has them registering less, voting less, and being otherwise less involved in the political process than older people are. Rather than 15 million young voters registering the real total was about 10 million.

Furthermore, among those 18-24 who did register and who voted in the 1972 presidential election, there was little evidence of monolithic solidarity in voting preference for the South Dakota Senator. True, the young did not divide along the overall 62%-38% landslide for Richard Nixon, but neither did they divide 4 to 1 or 3 to 1 for McGovern, a split originally envisioned by his campaign strategists. Poll data suggest that in the November election in 1972 they divided only narrowly for McGovern—on the order of 52% to 48%.

Expressed another way, despite Vietnam, despite the fact that they registered overwhelmingly Democratic, despite a host of other events and conditions which within some young voter groups in some areas would lead an analyst to believe that President Nixon was anathema to the youth of the country, 48 out of every 100 young voters going to the polls voted for the incumbent Republican President.

DESIRABLE TRAITS OF PRESIDENTIAL CANDIDATES

What qualities does the public desire in its Presidential candidates? Last year in one of our surveys we asked a representative cross-section of California adults to describe the qualities they feel a Presidential candidate should, or should not, have (Field Research Corporation survey on Presidential Candidate characteristics undertaken for *Los Angeles Times*. April 1, 1975).

We asked this cross-section to tell us first in their own words what kind of qualities they would like to see in persons running for the Presidency. Then we asked this sample to look at it from a negative standpoint: what qualities or characteristics a Presidential candidate should *not* have.

Does the public look first for intelligence or leadership ability in Presidential candidates? No! The quality named by 60% of the public, much more frequently that any other quality was "honesty, trustworthiness". Concern for people was 37%. Experience was 20%. Leadership ability was 19%. Intelligence and education was 14%.

The negative quality measure produces a mirror image of the positive qualities. "Dishonesty, deceitfulness" was named by 48% of the sample—almost twice as often as the next ranking negative quality they didn't want to see in their Presidential candidate.

If you jump to the conclusion that the 1975 survey results were heavily influenced by the scandal of Watergate and its aftermath, let me disabuse you. Public opinion polls for a long time have shown that the public rates "honesty" as the leading quality it wants in its President.

At a time when the country faces enormously complex and difficult situations at home and abroad, and when there is a need for people of great vision and intelligence, it is remarkable the public should have to be preoccupied with concern about simple virtues such as honesty in their President.

Burns Roper pointed out in a 1969 paper:
The public wants a leader whose words it can believe,
whose intentions it can trust. This indicates the
seriousness of the charge against a President of a
'credibility gap'. Since most people cannot follow all the
intricacies of policy; since for many, the issues before
the nation are hopelessly complex, since Americans
rarely rely on ideology to make their choices for them
and tend to vote more for a man than a party; they look
most of all for a candidate in whose character and
personal qualities they can rely on for wise leadership
("The Public Pulse" #28, January 1969, Roper
Research Associates).

An illustration of the public's priorities came from the profile
it gave the late Aldai Stevenson when he was running for
President against Dwight Eisenhower in 1956. In a Roper survey
at that time, Stevenson was considered to be an extremely
intelligent man, with good experience for the job, and belonging
to the right party ("The Public Pulse" #28, January 1969,
Roper Research Associates). But it is worth noting which
descriptive phrase came out at the bottom of the list: compared
with 45 percent who called Stevenson "a man of really high
intelligence," only 17 percent said he "inspired confidence."

In some additional measures on desirable Presidential qualities
in our 1975 survey, respondents were presented with a series of
pairs of descriptions depicting opposing types of persons and
each was asked, "Which of these two types of persons would
you prefer to have as President?"

Strongest preferences are shown for someone who finds out
what the public wants (80%) as opposed to someone who
decides himself what is best and goes ahead with it (18 percent).

The public does, however, prefer someone with above average
education and intelligence for the job of President: 62 percent
said this while only 30 percent opted for a candidate with
"average education and intelligence."

While most (72 percent) prefer someone with plain and simple
tastes, there is also a strong preference for someone who can give

exciting speeches and inspire the public (60 percent).

Most of the people (62 percent) feel the President should be someone who is ambitious for the job rather than someone who accepts it passively (26 percent).

In short, from this data it would seem that the public is looking for a strong, smart person, one not too complex, but who can inspire people.

The weight of public opinion is in favor of a married rather than a single person. However, most people say divorce would make no difference to them.

The majority of the public prefers the candidate to be under 55 years of age, despite the fact that just one president in modern times, John F. Kennedy, was under 55 when first elected to office.

In relating preferences to age differences, we found more similarities than dissimilarities between young voters and the rest of the population.

Young people also want a candidate to be honest. This attribute leads the list of preferences voluntarily offered by young voters. However, "intelligence" and "leadership qualities," are no more nor less important to young voters than they are to the rest of the population.

Young voters preferences for other Presidential qualities, such as the President finding out the feeling of the country first before going ahead, preferring a person with plain and simple tastes, preferring a President with above average education and intelligence, exciting people with his speeches, and is strongly ambitious for the job, do not differ from those of older people.

Only on the issue of whether a candidate should be single or married and whether a President should be under 45 years of age is there a noticeable difference.

Young people are less inclined to endorse the requisite of their President being married and being over 45 years of age.

It would be misleading to leave the impression that youth think and act no differently from older people in every instance. There is little question that today's society has been enlarged and enriched by the numerous dramatic and far reaching trends which developed in the 1960's, initiated by the youth of those days, and which today are an integral part of our social fabric.

What I am referring to is the whole set of values introduced by the student movement in the 1960's. Daniel Yankelovich summed it up well in a recent paper:

> The new values introduced by the student movement are organized around the theme of how to live rather than how to make a living. The stress is on self-fulfillment; freedom of sexual expression; less emphasis on duty, more on pleasure; a more relaxed attitude toward status as defining success in life; pluralism in life-styles; a de-emphasis on deferred gratification; a quest for novelty and excitement; introspection and the trip inward toward self-knowledge; a de-emphasis on neatness, orderliness, cleanliness, a desire to live closer to nature and to the land; a quest for variety in experience; a search for new sensations; a revolt against the functionalism and drabness of daily life; a questioning of rationalism and a search for the mystical and non-scientific; a greater emphasis on friendship and personal relationships; a rejection of formal social amenities and a more casual attitude toward authority.
>
> These are sweeping changes. As a result of them we are living through an era of transvaluation of traditional values of profound significance. Many of these new values were born out of a psychology of affluence now challenged by the possibility that affluence may not continue. Yet there are many signs that the new values will remain impervious to economic hardship at present levels, and that as a society we will not revert to the dominant Protestant Ethic values of the past.

These values are now embraced by a great number of people across all age groups. Of course, the ultimate results are never in.

SOME IMPLICATIONS ABOUT PUBLIC DISENCHANTMENT WITH THE OFFICE OF THE PRESIDENT AND OTHER INSTITUTIONS

It is not clear whether the political radicalism associated with the student rebellion of the 1960's caused or was part of a larger phenomenon of sharply declining public faith in our institutions—particularly the Presidency.

We are all familiar with the recent trend of decreasing public participation in Presidential elections. During the past 15 years fewer and fewer people participated in the voting process. Paradoxically, during this period perhaps more has been done to reduce the obstacles in voting than at any comparable time in our history. During this period residency voting requirements were reduced and we have made it easier for non-English-speaking people to vote. There was a reduction of the discriminatory practices which impeded Blacks and other minorities from voting, and 18-20 year olds were enfranchised.

Despite this the proportion of eligible adults voting in 1972 was lower than it was in 1968. 1968 was lower than 1964, 1964 was lower than 1960. Participation fluctuates and depends to some extent upon how "eligibility" is defined. But also upon the temper of the electorate.

What accounts for this variation and the *present* downward trend in voter participation *(Statistical Abstracts of the United States,* 1932-1972)? Is it the mood suggested by John C. Calhoun of South Carolina 130 years ago when he advanced his "concurrent majority" thesis? Calhoun suggested that for a democratic or popular form of government to survive it was necessary to distinguish between the "numerical majority," which is narrowly determined by those who vote, and the "concurrent majority" which is the sense of all the people— complete with conflicting group or local interests, including those who vote and those who did not. It is that kind of sense that might emerge from a rigorous attitude survey of all the people, with proper analyses of various segments. The error, Calhoun asserts, is to confuse the "numerical majority" with "the people"—an error that, by restricting franchise, could easily lead to tyranny.

The concurrent majority, in Calhoun's eyes, must always be acknowledged. It must act as kind of hovering, potential veto on the actions of government. Naturally if all the people did participate in some way so that the numerical and concurrent majorities were identical we would have a model popular government—but this is not the case. The concurrent majority is an essential mediating "negative force" concept against excess. A further interpretation of participation can be based on the fact that our system has imposed limitations upon itself. These checks and balances—not only the formal ones we always think of, but the informal ones as well such as public opinion, pragmatic party politics, caucuses, committee compromises, local elections and party primaries—all serve to mediate any tendency toward tyranny. And all provide a sense of reasonableness in addition to the concept of a concurrent majority behind it all. In this manner direct participation is not essential for all people in our system. There can, and often has been, the feeling that the elected government will do well by the people because its power is limited by complex processes, both formal and informal.

Thus Calhoun's traditional notion can be invoked to indicate a general trust in the process—or it can indicate a gathering veto. The question is: which is which today?

The fact that the public is currently turned off to politics and not participating may not mean that it is secure in its unconcern about what is going on in the City Halls, State Houses, or in Washington. It may be more of a feeling by voters that our political system is not functioning the way it can or should, it may be the growing "negative force" that Calhoun spoke of.

Calhoun advanced his thesis, however, at a time when the government had much less effect on the lives of its citizens than it does today. His thesis appeals to few today, perhaps because it seems *less crucial* to the process for government to be eternally conscious of a "concurrent majority" that is poised to rise up.

Today it is the people who are more conscious of government than in the past.

INFORMATION AND PUBLIC OPINION

Now, I would like to look at the impact of increasing information on the public's view of the Presidency. One of our long standing traditions has been the public's right to know. Therefore, we live with the assumption that people should be provided with any and all information which would assist them to form judgments about the policies of government. We have spawned a complex communication industry which spends tremendous effort finding things out, and letting people know.

Historically, the impact of information on the public has formed the basis for many of our earliest studies in public opinion research; and in addition, the idea of public access to information has provided the basis for lots of speculative thought on the effects of such access. I should like to share some of this with you with the warning that my use of this literature is selective rather than exhaustive.

One of the clearest articulations of the relationship between information and public opinion comes from Walter Lippmann *(Public Opinion,* 1922): "The world we have to deal with politically is out of reach, out of sight, out of mind. It has to be explored, reported and imagined." Lippmann argues, "The analyst of public opinion must begin by recognizing the triangular relationship between the (real) scene of action, the human picture of that scene and the human response to that picture working itself out upon the (real) scene of action." Thus, we have images of reality and images of images-in-action. Lippmann suggests on this basis that not only are the pictures formed vaguely by quasi-rumor, but that our actions are usually taken on the basis of information which has a character not unlike rumor. As he says, "Fiction is often taken for truth because the fiction is so badly needed. If we need to think of our leaders as heroes, or great persons, we will do so."

He concludes, "We shall assume that what each man does is based not on direct and certain knowledge, but by a picture made by himself, or given to him. If his atlas tells him the world is flat he will not sail near the edge." It is most important here to distinguish, as Lippmann does, between action and accomplishment. He cautions, "The way in which the world is imagined determines at an particular moment what men will do. It does not determine what they will achieve. It determines their efforts, their feelings and their hopes. *Not their accomplishments* and results."

An interesting question arises, however, over what kinds of information provide the best political atlas. Here I am deliberately implying that certain kinds of information may establish a better picture than other kinds. Clearly what the public comes to know in the course of routine disclosure may be quite different from what the public suddenly discovers as a result of extraordinary events.

In his classic book, *Social Organization,* written over 65 years ago, Professor Charles Cooley observed:

> Our government, under the Constitution, was not originally a democracy, and was not intended to be by the men who framed it. It was expected to be a representative republic, the people choosing men of character and wisdom who would proceed to the capital, inform themselves there upon current questions and deliberate and decide regarding them. That the people might think and act more directly was not foreseen. The Constitution is not democratic in spirit and, as Mr. James Bryce has noted in the *American Commonwealth,* might under different conditions have become the basis of an aristocratic system.

Cooley goes on to observe that at the time the Constitution was written the political thinking of the day held it impossible for a free state to be large. "A large empire," says Montesquieu, "supposes a despotic authority in the person who governs." *(The Spirit of the Laws).* The notion seemed to be related to the destructive delays in reaching decisions of governance of remote areas in a parliamentary form of government. Speedy decision was felt essential to the health of an empire.

Despite this theory, Cooley observes, democracy has arisen in the United States and in the Western world not chiefly because of successive changes in the Constitution itself, but as a result of changes in the conditions of information about the government and about the deliberations of politicians which make it possible for the public "to have and to express a consciousness regarding the questions of the day." The public has come to know things.

When the public is ignorant, public opinion has no power. "When people have information and discussion, they will have a will, and this must sooner or later get hold of the institutions of the society." In this view, equality of access to information has kept us from becoming an elitist state.

Is there another side to Cooley's picture? Cannot the media also spread distrust as well as enlightening information? A number of voices are saying just that. Media are seen to structure the environment in a cumulative way, and they leave an impression of their own as they transmit information to the public. Marshall McLuhan's phrase "The medium *is* the message", coined not too long ago, already seems to be accepted as fact these days.

In one of his wonderful books Professor Daniel Boorstin observes that what the public knows it gets second hand, and that under many conditions it may prefer to have it that way *(The Image: A Guide to Pseudo-Events in America,* 1961). He relates a story:

Admiring friend: My that's a beautiful baby you have there.

Mother: Oh, that's nothing—you should see his photograph.

Boorstin contends that since the "Graphic Revolution," and the mass media revolution in particular, much of our thinking about human quality and greatness has changed. "One of the oldest of man's visions was the flash of divinity in the great man. Two centuries ago when a great man appeared we looked for God's purpose in him; today we look for his press agent." In the last 70 years we may have misled ourselves as to how much greatness may be found among men. We may have come to assume that there is *far more than there really is.* But before the escalation of the media, people became famous slowly—the admiration, or fear, of a whole people was not built quickly—such people came into the consciousness slowly, as the result of extraordinary and consistent achievement and abilities.

As a result we naturally have come to equate fame with greatness. There may never have been a time, Boorstin adds, when fame was the *same* as greatness of achievement. But in earlier times famous people and people of great achievement were pretty much the same group. All of us, even our intellectuals, have a tendency to echo this idea that greatness is equated with fame, and that fame cannot be made overnight—it is a slow testing process. A few years ago Arthur Schlesinger, Jr. said we have no really great men. That the great men were in the past. Boorstin observes that there is a natural tendency to believe that the real heroes lived in an earlier time; and this simply supports the idea that it took a lifetime to acquire the fame of greatness—and one may not achieve it easily, perhaps not until after death.

However, in the twentieth century we have discovered how to manufacture fame, and according to Boorstin's analysis we have increased our demand for "big names" along with our willingness to confuse the "big name" with the "big man."

In Lippmann's terms we have mistaken our hopes for our accomplishments. But we avoid the day to day realization that we have pinned our hopes to synthetic products. Having made our celebrities, Boorstin says, "having made them the guiding stars of our interest, we are tempted to believe they are not synthetic at all, that they are somehow still the God-made heroes who abound with a marvelous modern prodigality." We are beguiled by our technology and our technique.

But "Celebrity worship" and "hero worship" should not be so easily confused, perhaps. By confusing them we lose sight of our real models. "We lose sight of the men and women who do not simply seem great because they are famous but who are famous, justly, because they are great. We come closer to degrading all fame into notoriety."

I contend that in addition to this confusion we have added sheer volume, which further combines the wheat and chaff. The public has more information about the activities of its Presidents than ever before. The comings and goings of Presidents are recorded and diffused in great detail. One by one, such taboos as the health of a President, the forms of relaxation taken by him—how much he eats and drinks, along with the language he uses in private, and his marital and extra-marital exploits—are all grist for the voracious communications mill.

But that's not all. We not only see the President, but we see the private details of his cabinet officers, Senators, Congressmen and their families. As television, the press, and accelerating public education stress contemporary events and personalities—until the truly gigantic figure is simply another face in the crowd.

Yet we cling to the picture in our heads that these are all great men, because we have given them easy fame.

Under these conditions what does full disclosure accomplish? Is it any wonder that research findings during the past 25 years demonstrate that TV attempts to present *full coverage* usually boomerang. This research shows that viewers, far from being enlightened, seem to be overwhelmed during the full coverage of conventions and other events. Instead of feeling that they are "in on the know," viewers often experience an uneasy feeling that they are being kept out. The full disclosure of all the bickering, the inefficiencies, and other human foibles seem to make viewers *less* understanding and *more* anxious. Disillusionment follows. The heroes suddenly have clay feet. A process somewhat contrary to Cooley's picture of information and public decision.

There is considerable evidence that since viewers bring little specialized knowledge to politics, even more full coverage of major political events does not allay this distrust. In fact, it may abet it perhaps by bringing even more pseudo heroes to the ruin of the lens.

Far from being enlightened and accepting of the information disclosed by media coverage of government, many individuals feel impotent, angry and hostile toward government and feel frustrated about the acts of their representatives. Moreover, full-disclosure seems only to confirm the darkest fears of those who habitually take a conspiratorial and sinister view of politics. Few people seem to notice or understand the majesty of the disclosure process itself.

These and other findings support the dismal conclusion that full-disclosure and reality information tends to be more often used by people with hostile views. Oddly enough, Kurt and Gladys Lang in their research in 1955 on political participation and the televised audience found that while distrust leads to a kind of withdrawal from the political process by individuals, it is generally accompanied by a focusing of their trust upon one, narrow, highly trusted medium of information—"which is somehow exempted from the contamination imputed to the mass media as a whole." It also places a high priority on a public figure who radiates confidence and is "sincere" and stresses "honesty" and honest talk. The conclusion is that those persons who are "most distrustful of politicians [become] the most susceptible to mobilization." Thus the public's right to know contains within it the mechanism for withdrawal from the political process through sheltered illusions and cumulative distrust. I might add a personal observation here: At the time of the disclosure of the National Security Council transcripts regarding India and Pakistan, I felt not enlightened or informed but, rather, I was appalled at the quality of the discourse among our national leadership. I was confronted by a conflict between expectations of how such matters would be handled by men of substance, and by the banal reality of how our leaders actually were handling them.

Full disclosure did not advance my participation, nor did it stay my anxiety. It made me sad, as advanced knowledge always makes us sad. Those haunting lines from Ecclesiastes returns again "whosoever increases knowledge increases sorrow."

It is no wonder to me that, despite the attention of intellectual elitists to "the issues," public debates and conflict seem to provoke anxiety or anger, withdrawal or hostility. None of these is good for the process, it seems to me. The debaters appear to be informed and assertive, but the public is not. Ambivalence must be the result. Frustration and anxiety arise over the conflicting realization that while issues *ought* to be decided on logical rational grounds, we see that our "heroes" in the unflattering process behind the scenes. Why should a normally disinterested voter feel guilty because he is uninformed when even the experts and politicians cannot agree either, and as a result of full-disclosure often appear to be equally uninformed or even fatuous?

In these cases the apparently well-informed debaters on TV are "unmasked" by more cynical viewers as unreal, cardboard cut-outs, reading partisan, plastic lines that have been well studied and rehearsed. Yet if the issue is complicated he withdraws; if it's simple he ignores it—in either case he relies on what he naively believes in his objective ability to "spot the real article" through the TV camera. In such cases the "real article" simply refers to some person about whom he knows very little.

It appears therefore that there is a difference in the consequences of full disclosure of information on an issue and information on how the process really works (or on how the actors really behave). It is this difference in impact on the public awareness and consciousness of these two distinctly different types of information that needs a closer look. One breeds anxiety and the other distrust. Both are disturbing. Is it because they spring from an unenlightened, but human, tendency to equate fame with greatness and activity with achievement? Or is there a deeper media process we do not yet understand?

I mentioned earlier that there are checks and balances not only in our constitution, but within the informal political system as well. All of our political machinery is filled with them, and during times of anxiety and transition, we would do well to preserve these mediating traditions.

As Henry Steele Commager has pointed out (*Majority Rule and Minority Rights,* 1950):

> Indeed it might plausibly be argued that it is one of the major advantages of Democracy over other forms of government that it alone can tolerate . . .dissenting groups because it alone has developed the technique (formal and informal checks) for dealing with them.

Of particular interest to me as one special and important technique has been the evolution of our primary election system. I believe the first advocate of primary elections was Senator

Thomas Hart Benton of Missouri who in 1854 proclaimed in opposition to the convention method for nominating: "I am for the people to *select* as well as to *elect* their candidates."

At first primaries were considered to be local affairs of little national interest. However, they have come to be formalized with rules and the status of regular elections. In addition, they have come to assume national importance and to be regarded as a part of the regular election machinery. As a consequence, recommendations are made from time to time on further formalization, perhaps to the level of a single national primary for the selection of Presidential candidates. I believe that caution should govern here because important checks would be abandoned, some of which will be recapitulated here.

During the course of this paper I have attempted to sketch out some of the possible sources of anxiety and security built into our system. These twin states seem to fluctuate from time to time over the course of history. But the evidence indicates today that we face a growing public anxiety toward government. Paradoxically enough a source of anxiety we do not yet clearly understand appears to be the media itself. We consider the media to be an essential, inviolable information-gathering mechanism, and we also are reassured to see that its tendency to arouse disappointment is *countered by other subtler checks and balances,* both formal and informal procedures in politics and government.

I also believe it is essential that these processes not be altered in a manner that could permit the diversity of our highly segmented public to be overlooked, neglected and further shut out, thereby releasing the media from their beneficial control. Perhaps our system of checks and delays has evolved for this purpose.

A single national primary, for example, for selecting Presidential candidates would be media centered, quick, and efficient.

However, can a single national event provide the same progressive exposure, healthy delays of timing, systematic trial and candidate diversity that characterizes the plethora of single-event primaries, all of which receive national media attention?

In addition, we are, as James Madison stated, a "Federal" as well as a "National" government. We are geographically dispersed, and the governments of these dispersed areas have separate and diverse views and interests. They are like a new "concurrent majority" and they should be acknowledged by candidates on the campaign trail. They should not be subjected to sole choice by a strict national numerical selection process.

Most important, separate primary elections elevate new persons and new ideas—as well as recognition of our diversity—to national importance during the several primaries as they are currently conducted. Such simple sources of new strength and diversity could easily be overwhelmed by the logical tactics of population centered campaigning during a national primary.

I would argue that *any* measure that might deprive presidential aspirants of having to deal with our national diversity first-hand or which focuses their attention solely on urban numerical majorities—instead of the new concurrent majority—should be entertained with great restraint indeed.

Some 20 years ago Clinton Rossiter in his book *The American Presidency* made an observation which has application here: "We should hesitate a long time before reducing a humpty-dumpty system that works with a neat one that will blow up in our faces."

5

Public Attitudes, Youth, and the Presidency

George Gallup, Jr.

Americans, particularly our younger citizens, prefer an energetic, honest President who they can trust, who is essentially nonpolitical and who does not veer too far to the extreme of the political spectrum. Youth does not participate fully in our nation's political process and cannot be expected to do so as long as politics is viewed as an "old man's game." A youthful infusion of new ideas and fresh approaches to old problems could regenerate our political system.

At the outset I would like to discuss the image of politics *in general* and then deal later with attitudes toward the institution of the Presidency.

There can be little doubt that Watergate sullied the image of politics and politicians in this country, but the fact is, sadly, the American people have never shown a particularly high regard for politics.

Yet in terms of survey data based upon scientific sampling—and this record now covers a span of 40 years—respect for politics is perhaps at one of the lowest points in our history.

1. As one has heard *ad nauseum*, confidence in many key institutions in our society has shown a decline. And politics suffers because of this mood of disenchantment.

2. Our most recent survey on the subject shows a smaller proportion of people today than at any previous time over the last quarter-century saying they would like a son of theirs to go into politics as a life's work. One of the key reasons given by these people is that politics—in their view—is "corrupting."

3. When we ask young people to indicate their career choices, a political career does not receive even one percent of the mentions.

4. College students, when asked to rate the ethical standards of persons in 11 occupations, rate politicians just ahead of advertising executives at the bottom of the list. Only 9 percent of college students rate the ethical standards of politicians as "high" or "very high".

5. Seven in 10 young adults in the 18-to-29 age group expressed the belief in an earlier survey that some Congressmen and Senators used illegal or unethical measures to gain office.

6. Further evidence of the disenchantment with politics is seen in the growing number of voters who do not align themselves with either major party. The fact is there are now far more Independents than Republicans. And almost half of college students now call themselves Independents.

Given the aforementioned, one could hardly expect to find young people fired up about politics. And they aren't, as indicated by the low voter registration among youth as well as their relatively poor voting record in the national elections in which they have been able to participate.

This is particularly unfortunate inasmuch as youth today, in general, appear eager to serve society. They have been called the "self-centered generation," but I think this is a misnomer. Many are interested in entering the so-called "helping" professions—teaching, social work, and the like—and a good number have already put in many hours working among the poor and underprivileged of our society.

Young people today show little interest in being the Chief Executive, perhaps not surprising in view of their turned-off feelings about politics in general and in view of the price one pays to be in the nation's top office—a brutal schedule, little privacy, merciless criticism.

Our youth today are further turned off by the traditional type of politicking—the bitter partisan attacks by candidates on each other; the candidate who tailors his convictions to the party line.

Americans today, and young Americans in particular, are tired of traditional politicking. People want openness and directness in candidates—character, not charisma.

What can be done to get youth more involved in politics?

One obvious way, in the view of some, is to stop making it an ''old man's game.'' Perhaps we have placed too great a premium on experience and have thus deprived ourselves of a youthful infusion of new ideas and fresh approaches to old problems.

Of course, it is possible that some candidate on the political horizon may suddenly captivate our young people. But whoever he or she is, this person will have to be a ''non-politician.'' Senator McGovern, you will recall, was in the early stages of the 1972 election year the hero of youth on campuses who tended to regard him as supra-politics. When his campaign reverted to traditional politics, however, his youthful followers deserted him. While it seems difficult to believe in retrospect, Senator McGovern during the 1972 Presidential campaign had a far greater ''credibility problem'' than did President Nixon.

Just a word about the so-called ''youth vote'' in the 1972 election. Actually college students overwhelmingly backed McGovern in the 1972 campaign, but non-college youth of the same age preferred Nixon by a substantial margin.

One of the basic reasons youth do not contemplate a future in politics is the staggering cost of running for office. Indeed, if there is a root problem in terms of the low esteem for politics today, it is the steep price tag for trying to attain office. To get elected and stay in office a politican must walk on an ethical tightrope because of the vast campaign funds needed.

Young citizens today are going to continue to turn a cold shoulder to politics as a career as long as the cost of running for office is so great.

Furthermore, it is doubtful that the image of politics in the U.S. will be much improved until certain basic reforms are carried out in the electoral process—reforms long sought by the American people.

The fact of the matter is, if the American people had their way they would revamp the whole electoral system—from the primaries to the Electoral College.

The new tighter limits on campaign spending are very much in line with the public's wishes. Beyond that they also would
—limit the term of office of Congressmen
—institute a nationwide primary system
—select the Vice Presidential candidate by popular vote
—shorten the campaign period
—abandon the Electoral College.

Surely our system in Presidential election years sometimes fails in its ultimate goal—to get the best person available in the White House.

There are those who maintain that "we may not have the best system in the world, but it works." The point could be debated, especially when one sees the sometimes interminable lag between public will and Congressional action.

This nation has many vital, dedicated, innovative and incorruptible men representing a tremendous range of fields and experience. Why do we not see more of them running for office?

Not so long ago, we conducted a survey of persons listed in *Who's Who* and asked them if they would run for the Senate in they had sufficient campaign money. As many as one-fourth replied in the affirmative.

Naturally any changes in our electoral process must be carefully weighed. It seems to me we should explore basic changes in our system and not limit our discussions on how to operate within the present system.

Shouldn't we, for example,debate the concept of a *Cabinet Presidency,* or government by committee, such as they have in Switzerland? It seems to me that this kind of an executive would protect against the excesses or miscalculations of a single man.

VOTER PREFERENCES

What do Americans—and particularly younger citizens—want

in their President? First of all, they want to be able to *trust* the President. Historically the top traits desired by the public in their Chief Executive are honesty and trustworthiness.

Americans want a man of energy and a man who does not veer too far to the extremes of the political spectrum. They want a man who is essentially nonpolitical. Actually survey evidence indicates that "barnstorming" and "whistlestopping" by a Presidential candidate may actually have a negative effect on voters. President Ford's popularity, as a case in point, hardly budged—and in fact, tended to drift downward—during the period last year when he was campaigning. I could give you many more examples.

Instead of the "pressing the flesh" type of campaigning, the public appears ready for a Presidential campaign by TV, with a series of debates between candidates on key issues, such as those between John Kennedy and Richard Nixon in 1960. This Bicentennial year would be a good time for such debates, perhaps including debates on national purpose.

How do Americans rate the Presidency? Only one person in five (23 percent) says he or she has a "great deal" of confidence in the Presidency or the Executive Branch of government. The other percentages: 26 percent express "quite a lot" of confidence, 38 percent say "some", 18 percent "very little", while one percent say "none", and 3 percent do not express an opinion.

Looking at the views of young people, we find only 14 percent expressing a "great deal" of confidence in the nation's highest office.

The public as a whole, however, rates the Presidency higher than Congress—and about the same as the third branch, the U.S. Supreme Court.

Speaking of the qualifications of candidates, the climate has never been more receptive than it is today for a female Chief Executive, particularly among young adults. The greatest bias women face, ironically, is from their own sex.

While voters today appear to be placing a premium on character in their Presidential candidates, issues remain decisive.

Even St. Francis of Assissi would have a declining popularity rating when the economy is sluggish or in bad shape.

Indeed, nothing has so devastating an effect on a President's popularity as do economic troubles. President Truman's popularity plunged 44 percentage points in just one year, between mid-1945 and mid-1946, largely as a result of the public's concern over economic matters. President Eisenhower's low point in popularity was recorded in the spring of 1958 during a period of recession. And all throughout the Watergate era, the public was actually concerned more about the economy than it was about Watergate.

While a lack of political awareness and participation among young people is to a certain extent expected, surely there is ample evidence to indicate that the younger members of our society do not play a great enough role in politics in this country.

So, in conclusion, I would like to suggest that, the great amount of attention devoted in these papers to issues such as the relative strength of the Presidency and Congress is possibly misfocused. Perhaps our greatest efforts should be directed toward ways to remove the barriers which prevent young people from full participation in our nation's political process.

Table 1

"Would you tell me how much confidence you, yourself, have in the following institutions in American society—a great deal, quite a lot, some, or very little?

	Great Deal %	Quite A Lot %	Some %	Very Little %	None %	Don't Know %
PRESIDENCY/ EXECUTIVE BRANCH						
National	23	29	29	14	2	3
Under 30 years	14	35	34	14	2	1
18-24 years	12	33	35	16	3	1
25-29 years	18	36	32	12	2	*
30-49 years	21	31	31	14	*	3
50 and over	31	25	24	14	2	4
CONGRESS						
National	14	26	38	18	1	3
Under 30 years	8	27	46	17	*	2
18-24 years	7	27	45	19	*	2
25-29 years	9	29	47	14	*	1
30-49 years	14	30	37	15	1	3
50 and over	20	21	32	21	2	4
SUPREME COURT						
National	22	27	28	16	1	6
Under 30 years	23	31	27	15	*	4
18-24 years	22	31	28	14	*	5
25-29 years	25	30	27	17	*	1
30-49 years	22	28	31	13	1	5
50 and over	23	24	26	17	2	8

*Less than one percent
Based on a June, 1975, survey of 1,626 adults, 18 and older, interviewed in person in more than 300 scientifically selected locations across the nation.

COMMENTARIES ON FIELD AND GALLUP ESSAYS

GERALD WARREN: I would like to key what I am going to get into which will be a series of questions about polls to something that was just said by Mr. Field about the primary system. Though I agree that as cumbersome as it is and as expensive as it is, a system of state-by-state primaries is a much better vehicle for identifying a potential President than is a national primary. And much of the commentary in these papers has been about people being turned off by politics and we are centering in the panel discussion on public attitudes, on the youth, although Mr. Field makes a very good point that we should not center on the youth as a bloc because I think, my view of it is that the youth who are not in the political system are not there because they haven't been asked by the right people. The youth are not any different than anybody else, they want the same things, they just have higher standards.

One of the things that concerns me if we moved to a national primary system would be the massive difficulty faced to identify a young candidate who is unknown. And this leads me to my first question about polls. I think anything that expands knowledge and expands sorrow to the extent of damaging the chances of a young unknown to aspire to the Presidency is dangerous to our system and I wonder if the media and the pollsters, my profession and yours, do not share some blame in disappointing young candidates by early testing of a relatively unknown candidate against a very well known candidate and I'm concerned primarily now with the Democratic primaries because in the Republican primaries you have two men who have a great name recognition around the country. I don't think that's a danger to the Republican primary. In the Democratic primaries, I think it is a danger. it seems to me when you're testing an unknown, a relatively unknown in New Hampshire, such as a Bentsen perhaps, against a Humphrey, you're not telling the media what we need to know to tell our readers that the people who are preferring Humphrey are really preferring him because they know him and they don't know Senator Bentsen, for exam-

ple. I picked his name out of the eleven now on the list.
Wouldn't it be a good idea in early polling of preferences for
candidates to add on a second line about how well people know
the candidate or the name they're being asked to identify?

I have been concerned about the depth of the emotion when
people are asked by a pollster, "Do you approve?" and he says
yes or no or maybe. How strongly does he approve and how
much does he know about the subject? I think our public opinion
polls and I'm going to continue to link this to media, and
particularly the newspapers because we use them, we use them
all the time, and I think when an opinion poll comes out, it's
probably very very complete and students could interpret it. By
the time it's interpreted for the average reader by a wire service
or a newspaper reporter, it sort of gets distilled and you don't
have that second line in there that I think we need to have—the
strength of the position of the person who's being polled, I think
the success of politics in our free system and in any free system is
to bring out the best person to be President, Senator, Governor,
or whatever and whatever opinion polls do to inhibit that young
unknown, I think is a great danger. I believe that some of those
things that have been said here lead to the inevitable question
that will come from the floor, I know, and that is the difference
in the polls, the variance in the polls, the recent example of your
poll, Dr. Gallup, and the Harris poll on Ford and Reagan. We
have a very volatile situation, it seems to me, in the country right
now with opinion changing quite often.

I'm concerned about the primary polling and whether or not
we should have different standards for primary polling than we do
for the national general election because after the conventions,
then both candidates have name recognition, even if there's an
unknown who comes up through the democratic primaries, he will
be known and he will be recognized after the conventions and
therefore different standards could apply. I think we ought to
think very carefully about how we poll toward the end of the
campaign season and toward the November election, whether or
not, I know you discussed this before in other places, whether or
not we should cut off polling two or three weeks before the general

election. I'm reminded of some rather significant swings in the polls in 1969, where after they had run 51-49 Kennedy or 51-49 Nixon, at least one of the polls showed 53-47 for Kennedy two weeks before the election and there really hadn't been that much happening. A great deal of time had passed after the first debate and there had been telethons and things like that, but there was no great event that I could recall to change that. Well, as we all know the election came out almost even. I think there was a similar swing in the 1968 election after very even polling between Senator Humphrey and Mr. Nixon, at the end it swung again to 53-47 for Senator Humphrey. This was one poll, not all of them, but one poll. Now correct me if I'm wrong, Dr. Gallup, but I think that would represent about 5 million votes in a national general election, 53-47. And as we know, Richard Nixon won by 500,000 votes.

It's apparent that polls don't affect public opinion, but they do affect the people around the candidate, they do affect the candidate's workers, his supporters, his financial backers, and they affect the reporters who affect public opinion. And as I know you two gentlemen are concerned about the credibility of your profession, I think you should become, perhaps, more concerned about the credibility and about how you do affect the national electoral process because it seems to me that everybody, every newspaper, every candidate in the country, is buying a poll of one kind or another and unless you are assured that everyone in your organization or everyone selling polls is very clean and very pure, it's going to affect your profession greatly and I think the impact that we should have on us, on the body politic, will be diminished greatly. I would suggest that whatever organization you have, perhaps you set up some sort of a self-policy apparatus within that organization whereby you can publicly point to those practicing your profession who are not doing it honorably. I don't think we have a danger at the present time of any more regulation of media, newspaper, television or of public opinion polling, but that is not to say that'll always be the case, I think there is a danger and you do not want, and we do not want, the government to come in and show you how to run your business.

KARL LAMB: It is encouraging to hear that the Editor [Mr. Warren] has some misgivings about the polls. I have some misgivings about both polls and editors, and that's what I want to express.

In line with what Mr. Field says, that knowledge is sadness, I want to report that a recent book by Ladd and Hadley (Everett Carl Ladd, Jr., with Charles D. Hadley, *Transformations of the American Party System)* makes pretty clear that there is no such thing, nor has there been such a thing, as a "youth vote." The authors considered the question of generational change in voting. When they looked over voters according to the year of their birth, they found that those who became voters at the most dramatic time of realignment in American history, the 1930's era of the Great Depression, did not continue as a separate "age cohort." The data examined consisted of forty years of Gallup polls. Their conclusion is that people of varying ages have the same kind of party adherence, and that adherence varies according to occupation and socio-economic status and all of the traditional variables, but not very much by age. So that we don't really have the phenomenon of the generational cohort of voters. So that if you all (the young voters of the audience) are thinking about a "youth vote," you'll be the first ones who have achieved it. It hasn't happened before.

Looking over the essays of this book, it is rather striking to discover that there is no particular discussion devoted to the relationships between the political parties and the Presidency. One immediately wonders why this is the case. An explanation of course is that the reality of partisanship is so obvious that there is no need to talk about it, that partisanship was recognized in the very planning of the papers that comprise this book. There are papers by political scientists, journalists, and others of both partisan persuasions. And we have a marvelous balance. I must say that they have found more Republican political scientists and journalists than I was even sure could be gathered in one room. Of course, having Senator Humphrey's presentation here gives him the last word, and that may or may not be wishful thinking on the part of the planners.

One of the explanations then would be that we don't have to talk about political parties because everybody knows about them. But a second explanation would be that, as David Broder has put it, "the party's over" (David S. Broder, *The Party is Over*). American political parties are dead, and we are awaiting only their burial. Of course the political party was a magnificent, unintended, and hardly conscious invention of the Founding Fathers. In his farewell address, George Washington warned us against the spirit of faction or party. What he really meant was that any faction or party other than the Federalist Party would be dangerous to the national health. Political parties came in with Washington and Adams, and we managed a peaceful change to the minority party (or the opposition) with Jefferson. At that point American parties, the first modern democratic political parties, had developed their modern functions. The most important of these is to pose the issues for decision so that the voters may decide between them. Parties do this by writing platforms and by nominating candidates. Parties also maintain organizations which are continuing enterprises and attempt to gain public office. Finally, of course, parties staff the government and take collective responsibility for its performance. This makes of the election a referendum on the performance of government. To paraphrase Walter Dean Burnham, the political party is the only invention of the mind of Western man that gives the collectively powerless a source of defense against the centers of power in society (Burnham, *Critical Elections and the Mainsprings of American Politics*).

Political parties are very important, and it is always hard to explain this to a California audience, because we do not really have political parties in California. We lack the kinds of organizations that are recognized as parties in Massachusetts, Ohio, Michigan, and Indiana.

The argument runs that the functions of those political parties are really being taken over by the media. No longer is an army of precinct workers necessary to go out into the homes of the voters and persuade them of the party's principles and the virtues of its candidates. This is really done by the media. You see the candidates, particularly the national and perhaps the state candidates, on television and learn the candidate's personality and his attractions through having him in your living room. The precinct worker need not knock. Of course the precinct worker of olden days might tell you about the advantages that could be had at City Hall through supporting the party too. Decisions once made by negotiation in the nominating conventions are largely made in advance now by the media, through the images that are created, sometimes deliberately, sometimes not, by the people for whom the drama of politics is more and more being played. Those are the professional observers of politics.

Even now, candidates are tramping through the snows of New Hampshire and journalists are busy deciding how much of a vote a candidate needs to win. Now if this election were only an election, he would win with 51%. The journalists are arguing, "How much does Reagan need in order to beat Ford?" The Reagan people said if Reagan gets 30% of the vote he will have won. The Ford people perversely say that it is an election and the winner will have 51% and anything else doesn't matter. But of course the professional observers are explaining the nature of the New Hampshire electorate and discounting this and discounting that. Most people forget that in 1968 Lyndon Johnson won the Democratic primary in New Hampshire. Of course, Mr. McCarthy made such a showing that Lyndon Johnson withdrew his candidacy after that. But in fact it was Lyndon Johnson who got the largest vote. So we have a paradox here, we have the primary election which is intended to make the operations of the party more democratic, allow the grass-roots participants of the party to get involved, and in fact it is being held for a private audience almost, the audience of the professional observers who will then explain the meaning of the primary to the rest of the country and create an image of the candidate which may be determinative. Thus it is the media who are taking over the traditional functions of the party in naming the candidate.

Meanwhile, of course, the professional samplers of opinion are also telling us about the performance of our politicians. The Gallup Poll's Presidential popularity rating is consulted like some kind of barometer or perhaps fever thermometer to measure the performance of Presidents. Here is the popularity rating rising or plummeting and this presumably is an indication of whether a President is in trouble or not. President Roosevelt was a little amused by all this. He had a great sense of timing. In the summer when politics slowed down and his name disappeared from the headlines, others would call on him to get busy and make some speeches and whip up some enthusiasm. He would say, "No, people will get tired of us if we make too much noise." But when the time came, particularly when election time came, he knew how to gain the public's attention.

The Field Poll has been cited as being a very powerful determining influence in party affairs. You can have, for example, a primary election going on in California. The Field Poll can announce that Candidate X leads Candidate Y by 20 percent. Suddenly the financial support for Candidate Y dries up. In the old days, finance decisions would have been determined by the party.

Well, it seems to me that this panel comes closest to discussing the second explanation for ignoring parties, that the party is over and that the media are taking over a lot of party functions. Of course, it is the media which publish the findings of the public pollsters such as Mr. Field and Mr. Gallup. Mr. Field and Mr. Gallup are impeccably scientific in their method. The science of survey research has become quite a definite science at this point. There will be no repetition of the disaster of 1948. Yet, interestingly enough, Mr. Gallup tends to be scientifically somewhat Republican while the Lou Harris polling organization tends to be scientifically somewhat Democratic, which is an interesting comparison.

Mr. Warren has said, "Why can't the polls tell us how seriously the voters believe in the things that they respond about?" This is the problem of intensity. Opinion intensity cannot really be measured very well in the kind of interviews that you have to do if you have a statistically reliable sample. The problem is that the subjects of survey research are also its consumers. Imagine a chemist who works in a laboratory with atoms—perhaps if he's a very simpleminded scientist—trying to combine some oxygen and some hydrogen atoms to get some water. Interestingly enough those atoms are not aware that they are being experimented upon. In social science, on the other hand, the subjects are often the consumers. When voters read the finding of the opinion polls, their own attitudes are changed as a result. It is as if the perverse atoms of hydrogen and oxygen refused to form a water molecule. Voters said to themselves, George Gallup says that Harry Truman has been beaten; by God, we'll show Gallup a thing or two!

Therefore the professional students of public opinion and the journalists who write headlines about their findings are becoming primary participants in the political process, usurping, or else filling a vacuum created by the retreat of the party from the party's main functions. The problem is that one crucial function of a political party is to take responsibility for filling public office, taking responsibility for government. I would submit that this is one function of the party which opinion pollsters and journalists are not yet prepared to undertake. They do not lay their jobs on the line if they make a horrendous error through their intrusion in the political process. They can take over all functions of the party except the most important one, which is responsibility.

All of this reminds one of the voters who said that in 1964 he had been warned that if he voted for Goldwater, the jungles of Vietnam would be defoliated. "Well," the voter said, "I voted for him, and they were."

The ability of journalists and opinion pollsters to intervene in the political process without being responsible for the outcome is somewhat like the system of tenure amongst professors.

I would like to add a word on this question of the new independent voter. Congressman Anderson pointed out the difficulties that result for the nation when we have a President of one party and a Congress of another. Parties by and large are what have made the Constitution workable. Without parties to provide a common focus of responsibility, the checks check too well and the balances balance too well and the result is stalemate.

Now, with the rise in the new independent voter, who is wary of
a party label, non-partisanship operates on the Presidential level.
People seek knowledge of the personality characteristics of the
candidates. They want an honest man, they want a person of
integrity, they want someone who can be trusted, forget the party
label. Then when they get down the ballot a ways, they vote their
party preference for Congress. What you can see coming is a
series of elections where the electorate thrashes around looking
for an honest man with their doomed Diogenes lamp. And
Congress stays in the control of a single party. Thus we have a
series of Presidential elections where there is no mandate. This I
think is happening, and it leads to disaster.

It sounds like the chicken and the egg question, really. It
seems to me that these developments are probably intertwined.
When the media and the pollsters take over party functions, it is
because the parties have abandoned those functions, or are they
doing a better job than the party? I think that is a very difficult
question of interpretation and at the moment I really would have
to say that I don't know the answer.

6

Washington's Two Governments

Robert D. Novak

Conflict between the President and Congress is a healthy indicator of our constitutional system of separation of powers and checks and balances. The problem of legislative ascendancy, however, presents the very real danger of Congressional government arising to encroach upon such crucial functions of the Executive Branch as foreign policy and national security. Continuation of Congressional enroachments in sensitive areas of Executive responsibility weakens the capability of the American system of government to survive in an increasingly hostile world.

I have spent almost my entire adult life covering relationships between the Executive and the Legislative branches of government and the last 18 years on relations between Congress and the President, including most of my time now, and it is clear to me that the institutions are in a period of very low repute. They used to say that Harry Truman becoming President showed that anybody could be President and Dwight Eisenhower becoming President showed that you don't need a President and now they're saying that Jerry Ford becoming President shows both those statements are wrong. But in case you think I am too critical of Mr. Ford, let me assure you that I feel very strongly when all is said and done I worship the quicksand he walks on.

Now on the other hand, we have Congress, which when I arrived in Washington 18 years ago was extremely inefficient, but an awful lot of fun and now 18 years later, it's extremely inefficient, and no fun at all. The problem I think now is that after two years of unremitting reform the asylum is being run by the inmates, and I think that results in a situation today where both the Presidency and the Congress are thought of extremely poorly by the American people but in a different sense. I think they still have confidence in the Presidency as an institution, but have a minimum of confidence in the present holder of the Presidency, Mr. Ford; whereas I think they have some confidence in their individual Congressmen but very little confidence in the Congress as an institution. This is extremely pertinent for what I'm going to talk about, because the subject that was assigned to me, legislative and executive difficulties in a time of legislative ascendancy, makes my blood run cold, because legislative ascendancy, I think, is a phrase carrying with it great peril to this country. And I believe that the American people instinctively realize that, from the standpoint of its distrust of Congress as an institution, quite apart from personalities and trust in the Presidency as an institution.

There has been, unfortunately, a great deal of conversation and analysis, by both the media and the academic world about the dangers of conflict between the President and Congress and the inability to have a smooth running legislative ship. I want to talk a great deal more about that; I don't think that's the problem. The problem of legislative ascendancy, I think, goes far deeper than the question of whether bills are or not approved and whether or not a President's program is put into action. The question of legislative ascendancy goes, I believe, to the survival ultimately of this system of representative democratic government and of freedom in the world from authoritarianism of either the left or the right. Our immediate problem is that authoritarianism of the left backed by tremendous military and economic power is gaining ascendancy in the world and we are but a small island. The question of whether we can survive on that island in a time of legislative ascendancy poses serious problems for us.

The problem in dealing with Congressional and Presidential confrontations has been that too often a President's record in Congress is confused with a baseball game or some other athletic contest. Too often politicians themselves talk about their records of percentage of bills passed, that is, that Lyndon Johnson was a very good President domestically because he had an earned run average of 80 percent in getting his bills passed and that was much better than Harry Truman who only had 40 percent. This is passed on I believe by my colleagues in the media and with apologies to Mr. Dillman of UPI, particularly the wire services, for their way of reporting Congressional news in the sense that President X was handed a rebuke by Congress today or President Y gained a victory in Congress today when in fact the question is really not who wins or loses, but what is happening to the public interest in these matters. For example, the 89th Congress, following the Goldwater debacle of 1964, was lauded as a great congress by much of the press and much of the academic community for its nonstop rubber stamping of Lyndon Johnson's programs. In fact it should go down in history, and perhaps shall, as the infamous 89th Congress which consented to a Vietnam policy which, whether hawk or dove, almost every serious student of history agrees was destined and guaranteed to produce disaster. The indigestible body of domestic legislation passed by Congress permanently added to the size of the government, the size of the debt, the burden on the people, and unfairly and perhaps disastrously raised expectations of what government could do for the people even beyond the level of those expectations in the Kennedy era when they were high enough.

Now through all of this there has been a supposition that it is wrong and it is undesirable to have conflict or deadlock between the Legislative and the Executive, between the Congress and the President. Lyndon Johnson immediately after his great landslide victory of 1964 called the departmental lobbyists together at the White House and gave what has become a famous little talk to

them in which he said, "Man and boy, I have seen every
Congress take the measure of every President since I have been
in town and we have to move fast before they wake up from this
tremendous victory that I have had." And that's precisely what
he did in passing this vast amount of legislation.

The idea that it is wrong and it is undesirable to have a
deadlock was popularized by Professor James McGregor Burns
in a book called *The Deadlock of Democracy,* which became
required reading for politicians and political journalists in
Washington and confused deadlock with the difficulty of
enacting liberal programs after World War II. Actually the
original function of the Congress, I believe, as set forth in the
Constitution of the United States, was not to rubber stamp and
not to approve automatically the program of a President, not to
be a bill-passing machine because a parliamentary system could
well serve that purpose, but to serve as an independent branch
and perhaps to operate in a direction counter to the President.
Indeed if there had been more conflict between Lyndon Johnson
and the 89th Congress, the good that might have been
accomplished, both domestically and foreign, could have been
immense.

Now there has been a presumption in Washington that the
Presidency is measured by how much legislation is passed and in
fact President Ford is now working very hard on a State of the
Union message which will propose a lot of bills that Congress
will reject. Ford's record on such bills will hardly be the answer
to his particular problems of leadership. And only recently has it
been suggested that it is vulgar and not very conducive to the
public interest to have a body of legislation passed without any
real quality but strictly as a measure of quantity. We are now
having politicians, particularly Governor Brown here in
California, but including others such as Governor Walker,
Democrat of Illinois, Governor Longley, Independent of Maine,
the Mayor of Pittsburgh, and the Governor of South Carolina,
who are not putting up heavy legislative programs but are saying
perhaps a small amount of legislation passed is more in the
public interest and they are finding it politically popular.

Even divided government does not really trouble me, and it may have been in the public interest that for 14 of the last 22 years we have had a government divided between the two parties as far as the Presidency and the Congress are concerned, at least as far as legislation is concerned. That the public has so voted divided government in 14 of those last 22 years may not be an accident but perhaps an instinctive feeling that that is the best way to protect the country. I am certainly not at all concerned by the current Congress and the current state of relations between Congress and the President as to legislative confrontation or the prospect of a deadlock.

Let's just take two issues that have recently been decided, taxes and energy. There is no doubt that if President Ford had his way on the Energy Bill, there would have been a decontrol of all oil prices and a return to a totally free economy in trying to solve the energy problem. On the other hand, if Congress had had its way, there is no doubt that there would have been a tremendous escalation in the degree of control and regulation and quite probably a Congressionally-ordered divestiture of corporate functions of the big oil companies. Either of those extremes might suit some of you, one of them might even suit me better than the other, but I think the mood of the people distrustful both of oil and of the government is better suited by the compromise legislation that was passed. It in effect keeps the present corporate structure of the oil industry while continuing indefinitely, although the bill lasts only 40 months, some degree of government control. As for the tax, we might say that the extreme positions on the tax bill were represented by, on the one hand, the Secretary of the Treasury, William Simon, and the other by many Congressional Democrats typified by Senator Hubert Humphrey. Secretary Simon felt that there was no need for a tax cut in the current economy and if there were to be one it would have to be accompanied by firm, inflexible reductions in Federal spending. Senator Humphrey felt, on the other hand, that we should be spending a lot more, we should be having a much bigger tax reduction and a lot bigger deficit. What resulted was that both sides playing the game of legislative chicken flinched, and where they ended up was with a tax cut. No one really wished to run the risk of completely eliminating the tax cut and including a rise in the withholding rates for an extra year while reducing the amount of increase in the Federal budget or at last making a commitment thereto to satisfy a genuine public concern about the level of government and the level of spending. It is a kind of an unhappy compromise but one that the public can live with better than the other extremes.

This kind of government by compromise is not very dramatic but it's not very frightening either. What would have been frightening in my opinion is a lack of divided government with Richard Nixon and an overwhelmingly Republican Congress which would not resist his tendencies toward authoritarian government. What would have been frightening would be a liberal Democratic president this past year that would have pushed out another 89th Congress stylist's dream of legislation through a Congress which was not very well led and included the most vociferous and vocal groups of freshmen Congressmen perhaps in history and if Lyndon Johnson in those fateful years of 1965 and 1966 had faced a Republican Congress, again, the history of this country might have been different.

What worries me about legislative ascendancy is not the meager product that's coming out but rather the possibility of the development of a Congress into a second United States government in two ways. First, through functions which are and of right ought to be in the Executive Branch and, second, by actually physically building what looks to be very much like the beginnings of a separate government matching the Executive Branch. Congressional government as described by Woodrow Wilson was horrendous but it did no great damage because we were in a period of isolation begun by Jefferson and because we didn't have a very big governmental structure anyway. Government was less important but there is no doubt that particularly when Congress, as it does today, possesses substantial power over foreign affairs the results are uniformly catastrophic. From the time that Congress repealed the embargo act of Jefferson, just about the time the British were about to capitualate, the tendency of Congress to yield to domestic pressures in determining foreign policy makes it a very poor initiator of foreign policy.

In that area there have been within the last year, in my opinion, more encroachments of a disastrous nature by the Congress than perhaps in the previous 20 years or perhaps the previous century. I'm just gong to give you a list of some of them, not in any particular order and not of equal importance.

Number 1: The manner in which the Vietnam fiasco was brought to an end by Congressional undercutting of the foreign policy of this country that saved not a single American life, because they were lost already, which probably cost many more Vietnamese lives and left us in the Far East in a very exposed and dangerous position.

Number 2: By cutting off aid to Turkey, by taking sides with Greece in the Greek-Turkish problem, Congress has effectively eroded an important alliance of the United States in the Eastern Mediterranean, perhaps for all time, and changed the balance of power in that important part of the world.

Number 3: Congress has, less disastrously to be sure, hampered attempts by the Executive Branch for an even-handed policy in the Middle East, by serving as the thin end of the wedge in the lobbying efforts of the Israeli government and Israeli friends in the United States.

Number 4: Congress, by its headline-hunting investigators, has destroyed the Central Intelligence Agency as an effective means of national policy for the United States.

Number 5: In the recent Angola episode in the Senate, Congress has served notice that the President of the United States cannot conduct the foreign policy of his country to confront brush fire occurrences, to confront Soviet expansionism. Though it could be argued that Angola was a very unwise place to try to reestablish a strong United States foreign policy and it may be that Dr. Kissinger, with his typical ineptitude at domestic politics of late, has by staking out a position on very shaky ground contributed with Congress toward setting a very dangerous precedent.

Let me assure you that the statesmen of this world, both the authoritarians and the democrats, are baffled by what is going on in Washington. They do not know how a government and a great power can function with two governments, a Congressional government and a Presidential government, and they feel a sense of foreboding for the future of the world. There is no doubt of course that the Congressional government in establishing its foreign-policy decisions operates almost wholly on the basis of domestic politics which is why it cannot conduct foreign policy. When Congressman Ray Madden of Indiana, the Chairman of the House Rules Committee, refused at one point in the Turkish Aid Debate last year to get a rule on a reconsideration of the aid cutoff, he commented in his friendly way that he had attended many picnics of his Greek-American constituents. If there had been more Turkish-Americans in the region of Indiana which Mr. Madden represents, the country might have been in better shape. But the fact that the Arab-Americans are badly outnumbered by the Jewish-Americans in this country in terms of numbers, power, and influence makes the establishment of an even-handed policy by Congress in the Middle East impossible.

Meanwhile another government is being built on Capitol Hill. Congress is a great deal different than it used to be 18 years ago. Then a constituent could go to Capitol Hill with a problem and be pretty sure of seeing his Congressman; today he is pretty sure he won't see his Congressman. There was a time 18 years ago, even 5 years ago, when Congressional staffers worked for Congressman X or Senator Y. Less and less now is that the case. Now they may work for a subcommittee or they may work for the Congressional Budget Office or some other supra-institution of staffing. There is no question that the staff is taking over more and more of the work on Capitol Hill and the staff is growing and growing. In 1974 the House Ways and Means Committee had a budget for internal operations of $500,000. It turned back all but $175,000 of that because of staff borrowed from government agencies that it did not have to reimburse. Last year, 1975, the staff of the House Ways and Means Committee, the operations of the House Ways and Means Committee, cost five million dollars. That is an extreme example but not an untypical one. The size of the government being built on Capitol Hill is awesome and one asks what in the world is it going to do. Certainly it does not make for better government because the House Ways and Means Committee again, to give an example, is still passing the same special tax legislation and perhaps doing it even more slowly than it used to. What you do have instead is a group, a new bureaucracy, built that wants to control the government and which I believe is one of the direct causes for the demands in the Pike Committee and elsewhere to see the confidential correspondence between the President and his executives. When you have a new Congressional Budget Office filled with staff, what in the world is it going to do? Is it going to establish a second budget and what will this second budget be? Will it perhaps follow the public opinion polls and go for considerably less military spending in an age when we are being threatened and where we cannot, as we did in 1941, ever catch up if we fall behind? Will it pass more and more programs which are politically popular and fewer and fewer which have no popular constituency? Will the Congressional budget process end up with such absurdities as Senator Muskie's equation during the last Congress of a cutback in national defense with an increase in the school milk program? There is no question that this rise of a second government in Washington spurred by the Nixon disaster and the Vietnam catastrophe is weakening the Presidency.

Senator Humphrey, who also has prepared an essay for this book, is one Democrat who's aware of it, who suggests to Senator Bayh and others who take part in this weakening process that if they get in the White House and I might say if he gets in the White House, they are going to be faced with the same prospect. Because unlike Senator Humphrey, I don't believe this is a pendulum process. I don't believe it is natural that this second government on Capitol Hill is going to fold its tents or the advocates of legislative ascendancy, such as Senator Cranston of California and Senator Clark of Iowa, are going to change once a Democrat is in the White House if that is the result of the 1976 election. Rather I think if Birch Bayh, Jimmy Carter, Mo Udall, or whoever is elected President will face the same problems faced by President Ford in dealing with some very unpleasant factors in the world and in trying to run a government that is not one government but two governments. I think it is essential that the Congress and the President come to terms in this aspect of their confrontation because what is at stake is not merely whether the batting average of the President is going to be 80 percent or 30 percent but whether this form of government can survive in an increasingly hostile world.

COMMENTARIES AND RESPONSE

LOUIS KOENIG: There are several themes that I'd like to venture to suggest as possibly emerging from some of the observations that Mr. Novak made on the question of relations between the legislative and executive branches. It seems to me that in listing as he did, and I think very legitimately so, various recent foreign policies in which Congress has been ascendant, if not paramount, that indeed these are cause for grave concern. The other side of the ledger, I'm afraid, and I regard myself as a friend of Presidential power certainly, is that a list too can be cited in which we have quite questionable action on the part of the President. Consequently, I would think back to the incursion into Cambodia, that very sudden move that had that strange history of results, the disastrous consequences of that, even today for the Cambodian people, as we think of their fate.

We can go back to the Dominican Republic, the dispatch of Marines as I recall in that situation and the picture that I've gotten is one of instant decision on the part of the President on the basis of highly limited information. The Angola point I think was put correctly by Mr. Novak as being somewhat questionable in terms of anybody's judgment, whether Presidential or Congressional.

In any case, the problem seems to be that we are in the midst of a series of agonizing decisions and the prospect is we'll continue to be. In other words, there will be surely more Angolas, more Vietnams, and each time we'll have to go through the agony of what we do about it.

Therefore, the question is, Is there an ideal structure of legislative and executive relations in these kinds of predicaments that have been in so many ways, as has been reported to us in these papers, so costly in terms of popular confidence in the government?

Let me suggest one kind of serviceable pattern that I think is derivable from the history of these relationships. The relationships as the Founding Fathers set them up, I think it is clear, have a good deal of ambiguity about them. In other words, the powers of the two branches are fairly substantial in the field of foreign affairs, somewhat vague, and there is some leeway for each side to broaden its interpretations of its powers as each side one time or another has done. Many have observed, and I think correctly, that what confronted the Fathers was a pretty slippery job to try to spell out the provinces of the two branches. Thanks to checks and balances, in effect what they did was to build a special structure for dealing with problems, which assured a kind of continuing contest in which the two branches would vie with one another over the distribution of power. There would be some kinds of ultimate checks that would operate when power seemed to move too much toward one branch and away from the other branch. In the sketch Mr. Novak very rightly has given, we see the power moving strongly to the legislature. The question then that we could raise would be, Are there forces that will come into play eventually, such as reactions of public opinion and disasters of policy, that would force power back to the executive and produce a better balance between the branches?

But the Presidential model that I wanted to allude to is one that I would speak of as a consultative model, an interaction of discussion and deliberation between the two branches. My argument is that at some point in history we have had important foreign policy made cooperatively between the branches, or through consultative means. Let me give several examples. Our initial entry into the United Nations is a model of the kind of thing I have in mind. Franklin Roosevelt was very mindful of the disastrous experience of Woodrow Wilson with the League of Nations and to avoid its repetition, soon after Pearl Harbor, as I recall, Roosevelt took steps to develop some concepts about the U.N. that looked toward the future support that would be indispensable from the Senate. Toward this end, there were set up in the State Department a series of what became known as Cordell Hull's seminars of representatives of the two branches. A small departmental staff went to work on ideas about a future United Nations. Apparently there were fairly regular meetings among leading figures in foreign affairs of the two houses and officials in the administration, including civil servants, and also scholars brought into the department during the war. I remember vividly several historians working on this kind of thing. But out of this emerged, as we recall, the overwhelming vote in the Senate for United States entry into the U.N. So this would be a type of thing that I have in mind, namely that the realities of the checks and balances—separation of power system are such that consultative, cooperative processes are necessary and invaluable and indeed at times some shining examples are provided by history.

Let me give a couple of further illustrations. Certainly the Marshall Plan is a model along these lines. And again it would be a story similar to the U.N.'s. Key figures on both ends of Pennsylvania Avenue, members of the various departmental bureaucracies, even representatives of foreign governments, and legislators all engaged in an elaborate process of discussion and joint efforts, and again the thing I think went pretty well.

There is one more example that I have to mention because it's quite germane to a couple of generalizations that I'm going to attempt. President Eisenhower made the innovation, and for a brief while it was a very important innovation, which was derived from a difficult type of situation, one that might befall the United States in the future. I refer to the critical situations that Eisenhower faced in Formosa and Lebanon. Eisenhower had very much in mind the experience of President Truman in the Korean War, who moved into that war under crisis conditions and by autonomous decision, and therefore took fully on his own shoulders the political liability of the war as it became protracted and public opinion grew disenchanted. This is the kind of a pattern that is apt to develop in future foreign affairs crises. Eisenhower apparently resolved not to repeat that kind of experience and therefore resorted on these two occasions to Congress for resolutions by which Congress would give its advance approval to actions the President might judge as necessary in the situation, including the commitment of our forces to combat. Congress was an active participant since the legislators effected some revision of the resolutions. Nevertheless, the basic Eisenhower concept was that if there was to be political blame and liability it ought to be shared between the two branches. Either crisis would likely be costly and therefore the better part of wisdom was for the President to take this step. I sadly grant that the subsequent Gulf of Tonkin Resolution in the Johnson Presidency threw much of the advantage of this procedure out the window.

On the other hand we have the War Powers Resolution of 1973, which somewhat reflects the Eisenhower approach. The Resolution has some difficulties which at this point I'm not going to be able to get into, but that resolution too has a feature of consultation, namely that as the President perceives a situation developing in foreign affairs that he expects might become difficult, in the course of that development he is to be in touch with representatives of Congress, keep them abreast of developments, and obtain their views. This kind of procedure, it seems to me, is in accord with the Eisenhower method. Again, I don't pretend to suggest any kind of blueprint that assures future happiness and comity between the branches. But it seems clear that the realities of the separation of powers and checks and balances system are such that there are junctures and I think so many of these foreign affairs things that have been and could be mentioned and predicted for the future are simply hornets' nests and it's better to share the political suffering. So this is our thing, the quest for kinds of cooperative action.

Involved in this, too, are questions of personality. Some

Presidents, I think, are by their nature peculiarly suited for politics. Without rehearsing James David Barber for us, I would think certainly of Franklin Roosevelt, Eisenhower, and in many ways Truman as being able to deal readily and easily with key legislators—for example Truman and Vandenberg. A little personality assessment, in the fashion of Barber, is appropriate on both sides of Pennsylvania Avenue and might help the cooperative theme.

So this is one thing. I would like to pursue it more but must desist because of time. I do though want to mention quickly several other major problem areas in the field of foreign affairs that are highly relevant here. One is the area of executive agreement, the making of new national commitments or the renewal of old commitments. We've had much unrest in recent difficult years as to what is the proper role of Congress and the Executive, and we've had the enactment of the Case Act in 1972, a modest law to provide information to Congress that executive agreements were being undertaken. But we have indications that the act isn't working very well. Good numbers of what appear to be executive agreements have not been communicated by the Executive branch under this act. In any event this also is a problem area when the principle of consultation and cooperation between the two branches is applied.

I would further say that, as Mr. Novak indicated, the whole business of Executive privilege, is all too often a road block to interbranch cooperation. It is a problem, however, that can be coped with. Mr. Novak appropriately mentioned Kissinger's limitations in Congressional politics and domestic politics. I can certainly recall other Secretaries of State in the past who I think would be more adept at warding off some of the political problems that Kissinger has fumbled before they become acute crises. Again, I suppose what I'm arguing is that significant consultative relationships between the two branches requires political sophistication and skill of a high order. In other words, I would say that being Secretary of State or President, and working in the field of foreign affairs, it's no longer enough to rank well with one's academics if one is an academic in the post, but that mastery of the arts of domestic and Congressional politics is the name of the game in the kind of model I am projecting.

The second part of Mr. Novak's presentation that I'd like to respond to in the sense of possible future definitions of the Presidency, or perhaps a redefinition of the Presidency, is the point that we've long been in the rut of keeping scorecards on numbers of legislative successes of a given president. It's pretty clear from the Johnson experience that he cited that the game does not end when the President signs the bills and they become law. It is now clear that there is little profit in playing the game in the future and the future then is the game so relentlessly played as President Johnson did in 1964-65, in moving measures through Congress, the Great Society program of domestic legislation. The really big job, and the toughest job, is getting implementation. In a sense the easier thing is getting the measures through Congress, however difficult that might seem. Now I would suggest that in the future of the Presidency whether in the concerns of scholarship or of the practitioner, we've got to concentrate much more on what might be spoken of as implementation. Let me suggest a couple of possibilities on that point.

One kind of image of the Presidency that's emerged here is a highly personalized and in some ways isolated office. George Reedy's book, *The Twilight of the Presidency*, is a brief and insightful summary of this kind of perspective of the Presidency, and it would seem to me particularly useful in dealing with some of the difficulties that Mr. Novak warns us about. All this suggests that because of recent trends, another kind of government is around the corner, that if Congress continues on its present assertive course, a kind of Congressional government will replace modern Presidential government. An alternative middle ground could be provided by concentrated study of the area of implementation, a consequence of which would be greater interest in decentralization and popular participation. The Presidency, I think, has come to a point where people who are affected by laws, who are affected by programs, who have to live with them, whether they are clients or those who pay for them, these people in the private sector must have an interest and deserve a voice in the development and the experience of those programs. The Presidency in the future must become more oriented to popular participation, especially at the stage of program implementation. Because of time limits I can state this only as a general formula but my further interest would be in looking at our experience with programs such as in poverty and welfare. This would get us more interested in the subject of bureaucracy, its limitations, and the President's problems in attempting to cope with it.

NELSON W. POLSBY: One thing that went through my mind as I listened to Mr. Novak's talk was that it's pretty clear that what is required to write a flawless constitution, one that gives the right results all the time, is to know in advance what the right public policies are, what the right choices will be far in the future possibly. Then presumably Founding Fathers can program for that. Our Founding Fathers without such a crysal ball devised a political system that reasonably enough would respond more or less and in a highly structured way to contemporary political preferences. But because Congress and the President were differently constructed and given different but overlapping roles and responsibilities in policymaking, there was and is bound to be conflict between them. And it occurs to me that Mr. Novak is right in suggesting that those of us who write about this spend most of our time admiring or deploring conflict without spending as much time as we probably ought to in thinking about reasons why conflict takes place. And it seems to me there are at least pretty good reasons why there is conflict and it's endemic in our system between Congress and the Presidency.

There is the problem of differing constituencies, the fact that members of Congress and the President have ultimately to appeal to different sorts of electorates. The differences between them, as people have noticed, have tended to diminish over the last few decades but the differences are fairly significant and do make a difference in the kinds of policies to which Congress and the Presidents are likely to be most responsive. Second is the different structural environment in which the two institutions do their work. One is a relatively unwieldy hierarchy in which at the end of the day one officer of government gets his way, and the other is a rather complex and very difficult to fathom and understand series of overlapping committees governed by such institutions as seniority and caucuses. The third set of institutional reasons have to do with something that I like to refer to as the differing time and career perspectives of occupants of the two institutions. Presidents have to get results fairly quickly, their priorities tend to be governed far more by a sense of emergency, a sense of immediate response, whereas in Congress there is a sense of more time to do the things that Presidents want done immediately. A member of Congress can reasonably expect to stay there for awhile. When a member of Congress is asked on behalf of a President to sacrifice some political resources in the President's behalf, the member of Congress has to ask whether it is in his best interests to do so at once. There is a sense also of the operation of seniority, which means in part the expectations by a member of Congress that if he holds still and pays attention in due course he will rise to a position of influence with respect to a relatively circumscribed area of policy which is a good substitute for the stability and longevity of the bureaucracy. If you are an assistant secretary of something you can look forward nowadays to an average tenure that is not particularly long, but if you mash enough buttons on your desk, you will pretty soon get enough answers so you will be able to do at least a piece of the job reasonably well. On the other hand, if you are a subcommittee chairman in Congress, what substitutes for bureaucracy, or has in the past for you, are the time and experience, the repetitive experience of seeing successive assistant secretaries come and testify before you long enough so you begin to get some sense of what the work is that you are supposed to be supervising the exercise of in the Executive Branch.

Those then are the three main structural characteristics to

which I'd call attention. At any given time, when we draw up a
balance sheet there's bound to be some justification for a claim
that one or another institution has too much power or too little.
Whether we share the view, however, it seems to me must rely
heavily on how much we like the policies themselves which I
take to be what Mr. Novak's remarks were mostly about.

ROBERT D. NOVAK: I just wanted to comment on Professor
Koenig's statements on consultation with which I certainly
agree. I think that it is one way to avoid very difficult
confrontations, but I'd like to make a couple of points. One thing
is that the consultation with a docile legislative body will not
accomplish much of anything. If you remember, the formula
used in the Tonkin Bay resolution was patterned after the
Lebanon and Formosa resolutions of 1953 and 1955, I believe, in
the Eisenhower administration. The other point is that if we
don't have a docile legislative body, which is certainly the case
today and has been for some time, there may be some question
about how much consultation is going to accomplish. I think that
Dr. Kissinger has done an enormous amount of consulting on an
enormous amount of subjects but it takes two to tango and the
Democrats in Congress are not in the mood for tangoing and I
don't think they're going to be in the mood for tangoing after the
1976 election no matter who gets elected.

Let me make one or two points on Angola in this respect. I
repeat I don't think Angola was a very good place to make a test
case of much of anything for a lot of reasons. Nevertheless let's
remember that President Ford was not proposing that troops be
sent there, he was not proposing that advisers be sent there, he
was proposing military aid to try to create a stalemate which the
far right decried as a no-win policy. Now this did not come as an
immense surprise to Congress, it may come as an immense
surprise to you that it wasn't, but it wasn't. The members of all
the committees of Congress which under new legislation passed
last year must be filled in on covert operations had knowledge of
the Angolan operation and did not become excited about it until

it became politically propitious. Once it became politically propitious, no amount of consulting could have assuaged their intent to create a confrontation. There was one moment when Kissinger and some other administration officials were greeting the members of the Foreign Relations Committee and the Armed Services Committee of the Senate in a long endless session and it looked as though they had about come to a compromise whereby there would be at least a token amount of aid sent to Angola with a cutoff date. Not that that would change the situation in Angola a bit, but it at least would save some face for the government of the United States as one of the two superpowers in the eyes of the rest of the world. Whereupon, the author of the Angola Amendment, Senator John V. Tunney of California, said, "Wait a minute, if we're going to compromise, I'm leaving," because the last thing he wanted was consultation and compromise. What he wanted was for reasons of California politics, too prolix to go into at this point, a little win with the left wing of the Democratic party and he got it. Now why he was able to do that when he wouldn't have dared to do that 10 years ago is that there is a different mood on Capitol Hill, which is the result of Lyndon Johnson, Richard M. Nixon, and the Vietnam war. And that mood is not one that would partake of consultation as a way of solving this problem. When the Congress is willing to sacrifice the power it has today to agree to consult with the Executive, the problem is solved indeed and I'm no longer worried. I think it is an excellent way for the two independent, coordinate branches of government to conduct foreign policy, but at this point, and I think for sometime in the future, only one of them is willing to do it.

7

The Ultimate Modern Presidency

Stephen Hess

The "Ultimate Modern Presidency" has been developing during the past four decades and has now become full blown. Characteristics of this modern Presidency include a steadily rising trend line in the influence of White House staff as Presidential advisers with a corresponding decline in Cabinet influence; increasing suspicion of the permanent government, leading to a vast proliferation of functional offices within the White House; and increasingly to turn the White House into a staff of "special pleaders."

Once upon a time there was a little white house in Washington, in which, according to a servant, there lived a man who "worked but three or four hours a day and spent much of his time happily and quietly, sitting around with his family" (Irvin H. Hoover, *Forty-Two Years in the White House*). The man was Woodrow Wilson, President of the United States.

I am going to tell something of the story of that house, beginning with a subsequent tenant, Franklin Roosevelt, who took occupancy in March, 1933. The White House, of course, is both residence and office of the President. In a sense, it can be said that he "lives above the store." But I concern myself here only with his office arrangements.

Of special importance is that Roosevelt lived in the White
House for over 12 years and that during this period the United
States fought a great depression and a great war. The
unprecedented duration of his tenure as President meant that
Roosevelt's style, to an unusual degree, shaped the concept of
the office; Roosevelt's concept shaped public expectations; and
great events shaped its magnitude.

When Roosevelt moved into the White House there were 37
persons on the office staff. Nine of them were of professional
rank. The three key positions were a secretary who handled the
President's schedule, another in charge of press relations, and a
third with responsibility for the President's correspondence. The
Bureau of the Budget employed 35 persons.

During Roosevelt's first two terms the White House was
basically a personal services unit, considerably bigger but not
essentially different from that of past Presidents. Since Roosevelt
saw the Presidency as uniquely a place to mold public opinion,
his need was for assistants who could help him in his symbolic
and informational duties, such as speech-writing and press
relations.

Presidents before Roosevelt did not "run" or "manage" the
Executive Branch from the White House, at least in the sense that
we think of a corporation as run or managed by its chief
operating officer.

Even during Roosevelt's Presidency there was no National
Security Council or Domestic Council in the White House with
responsibilities for departmental oversight. There was no
congressional relations office in the White House. Presidential
assistants were considered utility infielders who were moved
from one position to another as needed or the President's fancy
dictated.

While Roosevelt did not use his Cabinet as a mechanism of
collective advice, Cabinet officers still had the major responsibility for running their departments, proposing legislation, and
lobbying it through Congress.

At the same time, however, Roosevelt had the peculiar habit
of proliferating Executive agencies outside of the departmental

framework. This contributed to a diminution of some department heads' standing and increased the number of officials reporting directly to the President.

This also served the purpose of keeping subordinates dependent upon the President. It was a technique better suited to the needs of the Depression '30s than the Wartime '40s. As the New Deal groped its way toward economic solutions that had never before been considered within government's province, the heady clash of ideas and the heavy emphasis on experimentation were highly productive. But the needs of massive warfare were not as well served by improvisation and redundancy.

POWER TRANSFER TO WHITE HOUSE STAFF

By Roosevelt's third term there can be observed the first shifts of power to members of the White House staff—power, that is, that was not merely derivative of the President's. Harry Hopkins, who lived in the White House, was given diplomatic assignments that directly impinged on the prerogatives of the Secretary of State. Admiral William Leahy, also operating out of the White House, presided over meetings of the Joint Chiefs of Staff as Roosevelt's personal representative. Samuel Rosenman, the President's speechwriter, assumed a positive role in the creation of domestic policy, which expanded as Roosevelt became preoccupied with the war. These three White House advisers—with special involvements in diplomacy, military affairs, and domestic concerns—began to alter subtly the direction of decision-making. Some major policies started the formulation process in White House offices and moved out from there, thus reversing the traditional flow. Moreover, as Roosevelt's health declined, additional responsibilities shifted to his aides.

This accretion of White House staff functions was not part of a deliberate plan. The creation of the Executive Office of the President, on the other hand, had its base in the Brownlow Report of 1937, which Roosevelt interpreted as arguing for the President as the chief manager of the Executive Branch.

This new entity, an Executive office as distinct from a White House staff, provided a quantum jump in manpower available to a President, primarily in the Bureau of the Budget. Roosevelt was relatively meticulous in using the Budget Bureau for institutional purposes. Yet there were some signs by the end of the administration that he was giving it more personal assignments as well.

Thus by the time of Roosevelt's death in 1945, most of the elements of the modern Presidency were in place, even if in embryonic form. The President, rather than the Congress, had clearly become the center of Federal action and public expectations. Whether the growth of government had outstripped the attention span of a President was a conundrum that Roosevelt left to his successors.

The shape of the modern Presidential organization started to come into sharper focus under Harry Truman.

We see greater differentiation of staff functions. While Truman's assistants still tended to be generalists, there were now some aides assigned to such specific areas as labor-management relations, minority group relations, and congressional relations.

We see the building of staff in support of top Presidential aides. Such Presidential assistants as Clark Clifford, John Steelman, and Charles Murphy now had assistants of their own—precedent for the fiefdoms that would later distinguish the White House.

The distinction between Cabinet officers as policy advocates and White House staff as personal service aides had narrowed somewhat under Rosenman. But Clark Clifford's performance as the chief policy advocate of the Fair Deal was of a different magnitude, virtually erasing the theoretical line between Cabinet and White House in this regard. And as Clifford's success illustrates, in any conflict between White House and Cabinet the law of propinquity is apt to govern.

There was a further blurring of the distinction between Executive Office and White House Office with Budget Bureau personnel increasingly used to perform staff duties for Presidential assistants.

Two major new units, the Council of Economic Advisers and the National Security Council, were grafted onto the White House, providing the President with manpower for increased surveillance of these activities.

And we see a near-total public acceptance of the Rooseveltian concept of the Presidency. When the Brownlow Report came out it was greeted by such newspapers as the *New York Herald-Tribune* and the *Chicago Daily News* as a "dictator bill" and an "aggrandizement of the President's constitutional powers." When the Hoover Commission in 1949 proposed new ways to strengthen the White House staff, the same newspapers wrote of a strong, unified Executive as "a prime requisite of republican institutions" (Herbert Emmerich, *Essays on Federal Reorganization*).

Dwight Eisenhower, as befitted a former military commander, chose a very different way to organize his presidency than had his predecessors. The White House became highly structured with a staff secretariat in charge of the flow of papers to and from the President; a cabinet secretariat in charge of the machinery of Cabinet meetings; experts, rather than generalists, advising on a variety of questions that Eisenhower felt were inadequately handled by the departments; a very elaborate apparatus for national security affairs, although the chief foreign policy adviser continued to be the Secretary of State; a full-scale congressional relations office, which acted as a buffer between the President and the Congress; a press secretary who devised a variety of techniques for controlling the flow of news; and at the top of the pyramid, a chief of staff, notably Sherman Adams, to assure the proper functioning of all the gears.

These new offices added to the size of the White House. Yet Eisenhower showed that a large staff need not be operational, at least if balanced with tenacious Cabinet officials who had the President's backing. Indeed, the smaller Truman staff may have been more operations-minded. Still, as future Presidents would prove: the larger the staff, the greater the temptations to try to run the departments from the White House.

The combination of an efficient and orderly White House staff and unusual reliance on the Cabinet fitted Eisenhower's personal needs and limited objectives. The liabilities of the administration—the absence of a steady stream of creative proposals and the failure to recognize the boiling point of certain domestic conditions—have been blamed on Eisenhower's techniques of management. Conservative results were equated with a structured staff system.

Could the same system have been adapted to the needs of a liberal, activist President? The proposition was not tested by John Kennedy and Lyndon Johnson, both of whom simply assumed that it could not.

Kennedy promptly dismantled most of Eisenhower's machinery, including the staff secretariat, the chief of staff's office, and much of the National Security Council paraphernalia. Schematically the pyramid was replaced by a wheel with the President at the hub. In short, it was a system designed to look like Roosevelt's.

The White House staff did not wait for problems to work themselves up through the bureaucracy, but rather sought out incipient problems for the President's attention. At the same time the President had little interest in the place of organization in the operation of the Executive Branch. He and his assistants developed a certain disdain for its routines. Chains of command were sometimes scrambled. Cabinet meetings were rarely called. The "lesser" department heads had a difficult time engaging the President's attention. Ultimately, the Kennedy people came to view the permanent government as an institutional resistance movement, "a bulwark against change," (Arthur M. Schlesinger, Jr., *A Thousand Days),* as Arthur Schlesinger, Jr., put it.

Kennedy's system seemed best suited to crisis management. It may be, of course, that this evolved because Kennedy was confronted with so many crises. But it also appeared that crises were drawn into the White House. Crisis management, almost by definition, lends itself to an informal, intensive, high-level advisory system—the type of arrangement that Kennedy seemed most comfortable with.

The President's style attracted persons of intelligence and creativity to government service; the administration redefined some issues, particularly in economics, and promoted some new initiatives. Such are the advantages that would appear to flow most naturally from the Rooseveltian model of a personalized Presidency. On the other hand, Kennedy took the nation on a roller-coaster ride of successes and failures—the Bay of Pigs and the Cuban Missile Crisis—and when the Presidency was inherited by Lyndon Johnson, who retained most of Kennedy's advisers and shared Kennedy's faith in the Rooseveltian model, the end-result was to be massive and disastrous involvement in Vietnam.

The Johnson Presidency proved what Kennedy did not have time to prove—that Presidents can be too idiosyncratic. The continuing needs of large organizations demand a certain degree of predictability in leaders. This is particularly true in trying to give direction to the permanent government, but it is equally true in trying to avoid misunderstandings with other nations.

Johnson's skills as a legislative leader resulted in an extraordinary record of major Congressional enactments. This was in sharp contrast with Kennedy's record. It suggests that Kennedy's failures with the Congress were not a product of his Presidential model.

On the other hand, Johnson's personal style—unlike Kennedy's—limited his ability to use public opinion to bolster his position within government. In this regard the Rooseveltian model was far less suitable to a Johnson Presidency than to a Kennedy Presidency.

Both Presidents felt the need to become directly involved in all aspects of the Presidency that they cared about, which brought a more than normal quotient of minutiae into the White House, and—in Johnson's case especially—engaged Presidential assistants in more operational and policy-formulating matters than ever before. New agencies were added to the Executive Office. Responsibility gravitated to those closest at hand. Personal loyalty to Johnson became an overriding concern and some Cabinet members were increasingly treated with suspicion.

In the end, Lyndon Johnson turned the Presidency into a bunker and then handed it over to Richard Nixon.

NIXON'S NEED FOR ISOLATION

Unless one wishes to go back to the Presidency of William Howard Taft, a prime cause of Nixon's failure was without precedent: his need for isolation. A Greta Garbo conception of the Presidency is simply unsuited to democratic leadership, which must depend on constant personal contact with the other actors in the governing process. But Nixon structured his White House to limit his contacts to those with whom he felt most comfortable, his most loyal aides over whom he had greatest control; or put another way, he structured his White House to avoid contacts with those who made him most uncomfortable and over whom he had least control. The problem of the Nixon White House was not in having a structured staff system, which Eisenhower had proved could well serve a certain type of President, but in Richard Nixon having chosen the wrong system for a Nixon Presidency. A President with so deeply isolated a nature should not have employed a system that made it even easier for him to isolate himself.

Yet one also sees in the Nixon Presidency the coalescing of the various strands of executive conception and organization that had been developing since Roosevelt and that, from 1969 to 1974, produced ''The Ultimate Modern Presidency.''

Even putting aside the question of how Presidential precedents when pushed beyond the limits of legality importantly conributed to Watergate and the resignation of a President, Nixon's mode of operating illustrates the inadequacy of running the government through an overly personalized, centralized White House command post.

THREE FEATURES OF MODERN PRESIDENCY

Three characteristics of the modern Presidency deserve note in explaining what had been happening so gradually over four decades as to almost escape attention until this late date.

First, there has been a steadily rising trend line in the influence of White House staff as Presidential advisers with a corresponding decline in Cabinet influence. (The Eisenhower Administration was the only exception.) Under Nixon this reached the stage where his first Secretary of State, William P. Rogers, who was almost wholly eclipsed by a Presidential Assistant, Henry Kissinger, and another Cabinet member, Secretary of the Interior Walter Hickel, had only two private meetings with the President in 15 months. Roosevelt's Rosenman was probably the first White House assistant with a continuing assignment as a policy adviser, although he needed the concurrence of Cabinet officers. Truman's Clifford was the first White House assistant whose policy advocacy carried greater weight than did that of most domestic department heads. Johnson's Joseph Califano organized the White House into a systematic center of policy formulation. Under Nixon virtually all policy, domestic and foreign, was initiated at the White House. This has meant a serious separation of policy formulation from its implementation. It also may create more idiosyncratic policy, since White House aides often operate with fewer constraints and less feel for the realities of what is achievable.

A second characteristic of the modern Presidency has been increasing suspicion of the permanent government, leading to a vast proliferation of functional offices within the White House and to the White House doing things because the President does not trust the bureaucracy to do them, including spying on government officials and journalists. Roosevelt considered the bureaucracy too conservative; Eisenhower considered it too liberal; Kennedy considered it too wedded to the status quo; Johnson and Nixon considered it too disloyal. Each in turn created additonal offices in the White House to oversee department operations or to run programs that it did not trust the permanent government to run. Nixon's White House became a veritable "counter-bureaucracy" (see Richard P. Nathan, *The Plot That Failed: Nixon and the Administrative Presidency).* Blaming the bureaucracy is an easy way to gloss over the failures of government, yet running a government without the support of the bureaucracy is like running a train without an engine.

The third characteristic has been to turn the White House increasingly into a staff of "special pleaders." This trend began benignly enough when Truman gave an aide responsibility for minority group affairs, in a sense creating a presidential representative for those who were otherwise underrepresented in the councils of government. Then each successive president added other "representatives," until, under Nixon, there were White House assistants for the aged, youth, women, Blacks, Jews, ethnics, labor, Hispanic-Americans, the business community, governors and mayors, artists, citizens of the District of Columbia, and others. Where once the White House had been a mediator of interests, now it became a collection of interests.

All these new functions, of course, created an immense Presidential staff. Roosevelt's White House of 37 grew to 600 in Nixon's time. With the bureaucratizing of the White House, it was hardly surprising that the White House assumed all the problems of a bureaucracy, including the distorting of information as it passed up the chain of command and frustrating delays in decision-making.

So the Ultimate Modern Presidency was now attempting to create all policy at the White House, to oversee the operations of government from the White House, to use White House staff to operate programs of high Presidential priority, and to represent in the White House all interests that were demographically separable. This attempt could never have succeeded. The White House staff—even at its overblown size—was simply too inadequate a fulcrum to move the weight of the Executive Branch, which now employed nearly five million persons and spent over $300 billion annually.

So returning to the conundrum left by Roosevelt—Has the growth of the government outstripped a highly personalized Presidency that has to rely on the attention span of the Chief Executive and his staff surrogates?—the answer would appear to be: yes, it has.

What can be done?

My response is that we must get back to basics: we must redefine what are the tasks of the Presidents, those activities that they must perform and that cannot be performed by others. The corollary is that those other tasks—currently and badly performed by Presidents—must be performed elsewhere.

Presidents, for example, have made a serious mistake, starting with Roosevelt, in asserting that they are the chief managers of the Federal government. It is hard to find firm evidence for the chief manager proposition in the Constitution. Congress, in fact, except in the case of the Secretary of State and in certain emergency legislation, gives the authority to run programs directly to department heads, not to the President to be redelegated to department heads.

This suggests that a trend of 40 years must be reversed: Presidents must rely on their department and agency heads to run the departments and agencies; Presidents must hold them strictly accountable; and Presidents must rely on them as their principal avenue of advice.

Rather than Chief Manager, the President is Chief Political Officer of the United States. His major responsibility, in my judgment, is to make a relatively small number of highly significant political decisions each year, such as setting national priorities, which he does through the budget and his legislative proposals, and devising policy to insure the security of the country, with special attention to those situations that could involve the nation in war.

Agreed, this is a considerably more modest definition of the Presidency than our leaders and some scholars have led us to expect. Nor does it guarantee that our leaders will always make wise decisions. It is also a definition that we will want to rethink at some future time and under different circumstances. But for now, I believe it is a definition for conduct that is apt to provide more effective government services, fewer unfulfilled promises, and less alienation in our society.

To the degree that Presidents undermine confidence in the Presidency by overloading the center beyond its capacity to effect change and deliver services, the solution lies in a different set of reciprocal relationships between Presidents, Presidential staff, and Cabinet members.

Creating a more collegial model of the Presidency does not relate to ideology; a liberal or a conservative President could equally operate within this framework with markedly different results. But given the high level of public distrust in our institutions that now exists, these are goals that are not unworthy of a President of the United States.

8

Public Expectations and Presidential Leadership

Grant Dillman

The problem of the modern Presidency is one of bending to the necessities of the moment and then finding reasons to rationalize their actions. Because our resources are limited a President must confront that reality, make the difficult decisions on how best to use them and educate the American people as to the necessities of those decisions. To avoid raising public expectations, Presidents must communicate directly with the people as to what they can and cannot do to solve the problems of our society.

I'm not sure what a word mechanic is doing in a rarified atmosphere like this. The Washington Press Corps normally doesn't study Presidents in historical perspective. Our job is to put up with Presidents as part of the effort to report their day-to-day foibles.

Personally I haven't approved of a President since Harry Truman. And I suspect he might not have come off so well if he had been subjected to the same skeptical scrutiny as our present-day leaders. Or if he had lived in a period as complicated.

To understand the problems of the modern Presidency, we should try to understand the Presidential state of mind which has been one of bowing to the necessities or political temptations of the moment and then looking for reasons to justify their actions.

Presidents really did have it easier in Truman's day. He lived in what we now perceive as a relatively comfortable world in terms of domestic politics. The issues were fairly simple. Our basic worries were the Cold War and the problem of a full dinner pail.

There may have been arguments over how best to reach our goals. But there wasn't much disagreement over the goals themselves. Our leaders sold the Cold War on the basis of national survival. And given the behavior of the Soviet Union, most Americans were ready to agree.

On the economic front, Big Labor and Big Business both came in for their lumps. But again, most Americans were ready to support programs aimed at expanding the economy—and their personal share of the economic pie.

In short, Americans were pretty well united on what they wanted.

Contrast that with today. Our society is splintered over such issues as busing, welfare, racial equality, women's rights and the role of Spanish-speaking Americans. You name it and we're split over it.

There are tensions between city residents and suburbanites over who should pay for the services the cities provide commuters.

We can't decide what the CIA should be. We shudder at the dirty tricks of the past. And yet we have a sneaking suspicion that's the way the world operates and that we're stuck until everybody changes.

We don't want the FBI sticking its nose into our business. But how else are we ever going to crack down on organized crime and other forces inimical to a stable and decent society?

We want a credit system under which we can buy now and pay later. But we don't want credit agencies circulating personal dossiers designed to protect merchants against bad credit risks.

The news business and the courts are in a similar dilemma. We want to protect the rights of the accused under the Sixth

Amendment. But we also want to preserve free press guarantees under the First Amendment.

Our society is in conflict. We are skeptical about our institutions and our leaders, ranging from the President and Congress on down.

The future could be even bleaker.

According to a recent report of the Life Insurance Institute, we are headed into an era of economic turbulence and economic disruption in which the work ethic will be replaced by a slacker "somewhat different culture."

The Institute predicted the transition to this new, still undefined culture holds the potential for work slowdowns, sabotage and riots as people are frustrated in their demands to be insured against losing their jobs, family breakups, faulty medical care and unsafe consumer items.

That is bad news for Presidents. And it is even worse news for those of us who look to Presidents for leadership and solutions.

That may be a part of our problem. Perhaps our frustrations are due more to our own rising expectations rather than any serious decline in the quality of our leaders. The blame may rest more with our insistence on instant solutions where in fact there is none.

RECENT VIEWS OF THE PRESIDENCY

But before we go plunging into the future, perhaps we should look at how some recent occupants of the White House have viewed the Presidency.

John F. Kennedy, coming to power on the heels of the Eisenhower Administration, with its leisurely approach to federal problems, sought at least to present the image of an activist President.

He favored such academics as Arthur Schlesinger and James McGregor Burns, who saw the President as an instrument for overcoming an increasingly lethargic Congress.

After he was elected, however, Kennedy paid more attention to the election returns and to the actual division of power in Congress than he did to the exhortations of these scholars—or even to his own campaign promises.

Kennedy did not move on civil rights until events forced his hand. And he attempted to move school aid through Congress by the familiar route of trade-offs and lobbying. He didn't use the Presidency as a club to get legislation, whether through lack of will or lack of votes.

Lyndon Johnson, on the other hand, wielded the Presidential club at every opportunity. Many credit the strong tide of national emotion following Kennedy's death for the success of Johnson's early legislative initiatives. But given his background and desire, Johnson would have been an activist President in any case.

Johnson destroyed his mandate by insisting on having his way—and then by miscalculating the effect of Vietnam on the public. His image as a strong, steady leader finally blurred in the public eye. And when it came back into focus, it was as a dictator figure.

It was then that people such as Schlesinger began moving away from Johnson. When the demonstrations erupted against the war, other liberals began questioning the accepted verities of the 1960's, including the wisdom of an activist President.

Richard Nixon completed the process as far as the liberals were concerned. When they called for a strong president in the 1950's, liberals viewed the office as a vehicle for action in behalf of all the people. They saw Nixon as an acutely sensitive politician acting for a favored few.

It was their own vision turned inside out and they immediately began clamoring for checks and balances, the same cry raised by conservatives during Franklin D. Roosevelt's Presidencies.

The liberals put their money on Congress to redress the balance of power. But they neglected the reality, which was that Congress was so encrusted with self-serving rules and traditions that it could do little more than react to Presidential initiatives.

Recent Congressional reforms have loosened Congress up a little. They have not removed the brakes that slow Congress down or sometimes keep it from acting at all on highly controversial matters.

As a result, we still have a strong Presidency, although a relatively weak President. It may be that Ford scared himself with the reaction to his pardon of Richard Nixon and decided, subconsciously or otherwise, that he wanted to share the hard decisions with Congress.

In any case, he seems to shy away from using the Presidency to its limits, at least in the domestic area, with the result that he frequently appears indecisive or blundering.

Even so, given the relative inability of Congress to act swiftly, and the temper of the public, which yearns openly for sturdy, no-nonsense Truman, or even an Eisenhower father figure, the ingredients are there for a strong President—if only we could find a Johnson with style and grace.

That would not automatically insure a successful Presidency, however.

OMNISCIENT PRESIDENTS

I referred earlier to our rising expectations where our national leaders are concerned. I don't know where it began—possibly with FDR—but we have come to expect our Presidents to be all-wise and all-knowing, capable of coming up with instant solutions.

Sometime someone must start telling the American people that not all problems can be solved instantly. Or even solved at all. Some, like inflation, can only be tempered.

Like it or not, we never again will get as big a share of the world's goods—or even our own goods—as we did in the past. Nations with critical raw materials are starting to withhold them from world markets to build up their own economies.

Other nations, as they become more prosperous—or desperate, as the case may be—are willing to pay whatever is necessary for U.S. products. Imagine where domestic grain prices would be today were it not for Soviet purchases, and gifts and loans to needy nations such as India.

Still we look to the President for a magic formula that will allow us to ship vast amounts of grain overseas to still keep a lid on domestic food prices. Worse, Presidents try to convey the impression they can do it. When they can't, it deepens the air of skepticism and cynicism about the quality of leadership.

Presidents must start coming clean on what they can and can't do. This is not a new problem. Past Presidents have pledged to erase poverty, eliminate crime, provide jobs for everyone who wants one, assure decent housing for all, establish a minimum income floor and guarantee health care for all Americans.

We need only look around to see what happened to those pledges.

That brings us to another blunt fact. Because our resources are limited, and becoming more so relative to population, we must face up to some hard decisions on how to use them. Sometime, a President—or someone who wants to be President—will have to level with us on that score.

Congress shares responsibility in this area, of course. Like our recent Presidents, Congress approaches virtually every problem with the idea that a little federal money can set things right. Our experience with crime, housing and poverty shows how wrong that concept can be.

Such shotgun approaches only succeed in diluting our efforts to the point that they are not effective in any area.

Perhaps Americans are ready for a President who is willing to forego grandiose visions of a perfect society in favor of solving a few of our more urgent problems. A President who could accomplish something lasting in the area of crime, for example, would go down in history.

Earlier in his Administration, President Ford talked a little about hard choices. We haven't heard much on that score lately, however, and we'll probably hear less as we get deeper into the election year. And I doubt we'll hear much from the Democratic side either.

Politicians share one thing with the media. They are in danger of getting their heads chopped off for bearing bad news. The media has to go ahead anyway. Politicians frequently find it advisable to trim their sails to the prevailing winds.

RESTRUCTURING GOVERNMENT

The President also is a victim of the federal structure, particularly our archaic Cabinet structure. It once was possible for the Agriculture Department to pretty much look out for the interest of farmers. Or for the Labor Department to protect the interests of workers.

No more. The issues affecting our everyday lives are so complex and diverse they sometimes spill over into a dozen federal departments and agencies. These departments and agencies need to be restructured to concentrate responsibility in a single agency as much as possible.

United Press International is ahead of government in that respect. We once assigned reporters to specific departments where they staked themselves out in the pressroom. The more enterprising of them tried to develop stories in other areas as well. Some just waited for news to happen.

Now we assign reporters by area: consumer affairs, energy, environment, national security, welfare, education, and so on. They follow wherever the story leads—the White House, Congress or some federal agency. As a result, our stories are more authoritative and more likely to reflect what actually is going on.

The government could take a lesson from our approach. In the process, it also should conduct an agonizing reappraisal—to borrow a term from John Foster Dulles—as to whether we need all the agencies the bureaucrats say we do. And if we do, whether they need be so large.

Maybe Presidents could be more effective, and government more responsive, if we cleaned out the cluttered attic we call government.

I also would like to see the Cabinet regain some of the power it once held. Much of their original authority has gravitated to 1600 Pennsylvania Avenue because the diffusion of power has made it necessary for someone to call the shots.

That "someone" usually turns out to be the White House, frequently resulting in the anomaly of a White House functionary, who is not accountable to Congress, overruling a

Cabinet member who is. That would not occur if government were restructured to centralize authority over a specific area in a specific agency.

There have been attempts in this direction. Lyndon Johnson and Richard Nixon wanted to merge the Commerce and Labor Departments. Nothing came of it. Nixon also sought to leapfrog classic departmental lines in setting up the federal energy program.

He wanted to take the energy and natural resources responsibilities away from the Atomic Energy Commission, the Interior Department and several other agencies and give them to a new Cabinet-level department. Moves were made in that direction. But six agencies still call the energy shots.

One of the problems faced by reformers in their efforts to reorganize government is the reluctance of some ranking members of Congress—committee chairmen and those who hope to be—to give up their little private fiefdoms.

If the government were restructured, the Congressional committee system likewise would have to be overhauled along similar lines. Some congressmen would lose their chairmanships. Many waited years to achieve their present eminence and they don't want to give it up.

The federal government has become so sprawling that no President can be in total control. Every President who has come to power in the last 25 years has done so with a promise of a federal housecleaning. The Presidents are gone. The bureaucrats remain, doing business as usual.

Congress also is unable to grapple effectively with the problems of big government. Few members fully understand the bills on which they vote, let alone have an overall grasp of the government. Lawmaking all too often is a matter of trial and error with taxpayers picking up the cost.

I participated in another Presidential seminar held at Harvard by the Roscoe Pound Foundation. There was almost unanimous agreement that Congress is at a great disadvantage in dealing with White House proposals because it is dependent on White House information.

Congress desperately needs its own information clearing house so it can form truly independent judgments on the wisdom of Administration proposals.

Senator Russell B. Long of Louisiana pointed out the problem last year when he was trying to rush a tax cut bill through the Senate Finance Committee. As Long's deadline for action approached, and with several members still asking questions, Long observed:

"If all the Senators insist on knowing what's in this bill, we'll never get it out by Monday." The bill was ready on Monday.

True, the Library of Congress is busy in this area. But its resources are limited. Too, some Congressmen have staff experts in various government areas. That also can be abused. The Congressman can use his data to help or hurt a bill, depending on whether he favors it or not.

One answer would be to overhaul and expand the General Accounting Office, which already acts as a congressional watchdog on government programs. It could be given responsibility for operating a computerized information bank available to all members.

It would be expensive. But it would enable Congressmen to cast more informed votes—and probably save money in the long run.

Given the divisions in our nation, it may be, of course, that all the proposals advanced here in these papers still would not produce a Presidency able to cope with the rapidly changing challenges of the modern world.

I hate to mention it in this Bicentennial Year, when patriotic juices are running so strong, but it may even be that we someday will have to consider borrowing a modified form of parliamentary government from our British cousins.

That would be one way of preventing members of Congress from rushing off in all directions, as they sometimes now do, depending on which way they think the political winds are blowing at home.

Party responsibility would have avoided the impasse between Congress and the White House over aid to Turkey and more recently, the bitter infighting over whether the United States should counter Soviet intervention in Angola by helping the pro-American faction there.

It would be anathema, however, to the many Americans who believe the great virtue of our system of checks and balances is that it sometimes prevents the federal government from rushing pell-mell into dangerous or undesirable programs or actions.

The basic question then, given the volatile state of the world, is whether we can afford Presidents who act on the basis of expediency or convenience and then seek ways to rationalize their actions.

9

National Policy and Crisis Management

Stephen Horn

The last quarter of this century is likely to see an increasing need for crisis management and growing policy conflicts as a result of political party fragmentation. The key to a successful President is the use of will. If he is there simply to be loved, he should not be in Office. Solutions to the coming crises and conflicts will best come from an institutionalization of the executive process rather than from ad hoc responses to issues.

I am bothered by the longing for consensus as a basis for the functioning of the Presidency and Congress. I doubt that we have ever had the consensus in this country for which many dream or wish. What we have is more extensive media coverage of the conflicts that exist in our society—conflicts that have existed from the very beginning of the American society and at times have been much greater than they are now and much greater than seemingly they were during the Vietnamese conflict. The media cover the conflict in which men or women engage, not the good they do. You see this on the evening TV news or when the newspapers arrive at your breakfast table. You see this with the search for the unusual what I would call the "klutz" syndrome where you see statements picked up that can demolish a candidate such as a George Romney or an Edmund Muskie or scenes photographed of a President Ford falling on the ski slopes. As we become more educated as a society, we seem to be increasingly concerned with the self-flagellation of the affluent. With our greater means of communication this seems to be evident in the focus of the coverage of desegregation in Boston and other controversies—all of which conditions Congressional-Presidential response to what should be fundamental governmental decisions.

As I listened to the descriptions of JFK and LBJ and their relations to Congress, and having lived through that period on Capitol Hill, I think it was generally an accurate one, with one exception—the fundamental difference between John F. Kennedy and Lyndon Johnson is that with the 89th Congress in 1965, the Democrats, thanks to Senator Goldwater, had two-thirds control of the House and Senate. Only later did some of the cracks show.

The role of political party, as Professor Lamb has noted, has been downplayed, yet I think it is basic. There is still a feeling of party when those with whom you are allied are in control of the Executive Branch and its departments and dominate the informal relationships that exist within the Washington legislative community. One problem, as Mr. Hess noted, is the permanent government, the bureaucracy—which I might add exists both on Capitol Hill as well as in downtown Washington. If there is to be political responsibility, then political parties must have the skilled individuals who are knowledgeable about government and who, when a President receives a mandate (even if it is only by a half percent of the total vote from the people), will go to Washington to help in the implementation of Presidential policies and what the people presumably expected to be done. That has not been done. Both parties have failed in this respect, although there has been a smattering of the so-called in-and-outers in both parties. The Hoover Commission made a very wise recommendation, which neither political party has systematically implemented, and that is to attract at the beginning of an administration younger people as assistants to Cabinet officers and junior assistants in the White House staff.

Then later as the party continues in or returns to power, perhaps 8, 12 years later, they would become assistant secretaries, undersecretaries, etc.

Over the years we have heard of the changing balance of power between the Congress and the President. We recall that periods of a strong Presidency—be it Jefferson or Jackson—have often been followed by much weaker Presidents. I suspect there might be something in human organization which causes such oscillation as the tolerant points build up when rapid changes occur and resentments obviously arise.

Then the view is well known among political scientists, as Professor Fenno has so well articulated, that the typical citizen seems to dislike and distrust Congress but likes or loves his or her own Congressman. He or she seems to be different than the others in Washington and that is one of the problems if you try to put together what is political opinion at the local level and have it percolate toward Washington and through an institutional system of representative government as expressed by the Congress and in the Presidency.

But on the Congress' behalf, I would recall that many program ideas of the Kennedy administration were formulated in the Congresses of the 1950's and early 1960's, and in both the Republican and Democratic parties. Many of the domestic ideas of the Kennedy and Johnson administrations did not originate with a bright young Harvard braintruster assigned to the White House staff to think great thoughts. The fact is that these options, be it Medicare or civil rights, had been battled over for a decade on Capitol Hill by staff and representatives of both parties in both Houses. Often it was those in Congress who were forcing the White House to act. This was certainly true in the Kennedy period, where they did very little if anything on civil rights until their hand was repeatedly forced.

One of the problems with Congress today is that the legislative branch is fragmented and its members have very little faith in their own leaders. It is doubtful if Congress could have leaders in the tradition of Lyndon Johnson and Sam Rayburn. A close look at that era would cause us to question the degree to which even

Johnson and Rayburn showed strength in some Congressional operations. Given the increased societal fragmentation, even if Johnson and Rayburn were alive and leading today, it is doubtful that they could influence Congress as perhaps they did in the 1950's when they could reach a bipartisan agreement with Dwight D. Eisenhower, their fellow Texan who was in the White House. Today Congressional committees are even more fragmented. A rare exception is the Joint Committee on Atomic Energy which has functioned very well since the close of the Second World War. Members of both parties who serve on the joint committee generally maintain confidences and have a close liaison with the executive administration in that area. There is another problem on Capitol Hill which I alluded to earlier and that is the rising number of Congressional staff. As a former Congressional staff member who takes great pride in and worked to improve the quality of the staff on the Hill, I would say we are getting to the point where enough is enough. The question in terms of monitoring an Executive Branch—just as Mr. Hess has pointed out in terms of White House operations—is not how many people you have, but what they ask, what they say, and what they do. Quantity is often destructive in carrying out those purposes. The tendency of any staff person in an executive or legislative bureaucracy is to justify his or her existence through the writing of more memoranda, many of which do not need to be written and many of which simply clog the information lines and systems and prevent clear-cut decision or the formulation of a clear-cut decision. As you can see, I am dubious in terms of both the legislative and executive bureaucracy. I am often reminded of Jefferson's comment that "few die and none resign" as he looked at the very small civil service of his day. And we all know the role of the Congressional subcommittee chairmen and the departmental bureau chiefs who are in power for 10 or 20 years—as many of them are—and the problems which any President, whether liberal or conservative, Democrat or Republican—has in coming to Washington for what becomes a very short period of time and trying to impose his will on the executive and legislative branches. I think Mr. Hess described very well the role of an executive. I would add to it several factors.

CONTRIBUTIONS TO EXECUTIVE SUCCESS

I believe that the key to any successful executive is the use of will. If you are simply there to be loved, you should not be there. Yet, most who seek election want to be re-elected. As we begin our third century and we begin the last fourth of this century and given the complexity and crises which this nation faces, one might well ask: can we afford to have a system where a President cannot simply do his best as he sees the light to do his best at the time, but must consciously and continually remember that if he wants to run for re-election he can only go so far? You have recently witnessed a rather dramatic case of this when President Ford vetoed the common situs picketing legislation. That is an issue which has kicked around Congress for two decades, an issue toward which President Ford was at one point apparently favorably inclined (I suspect because of the impact of the buildings trades workers); but when the more parochial concerns of a primary with Mr. Reagan in New Hampshire came to the fore, you saw the results.

Certainly another factor any chief executive confronts is his use of time. There is only so much time in the day and the question is: what do you do with it? Then there is the problem of Presidential style. There are many different methods which can be successful, different types of personalities, and different timing that might be appropriate given that collection of personalities. No executive functions in a vacuum.

Mr. Hess' comments on the Eisenhower staff and cabinet secretariat were well taken. To assure his own place in history, Mr. Kennedy would have done well to have listened more to some of President Eisenhower's assistants who had functioned in the White House rather than to Professor Neustadt, who looked at the White House from afar. Presidential power is of little effect without the coordinative and monitoring system to carry it out.

Still another factor is the listening function. How does an

executive find out what is happening? Mr. Hess noted the problem of a President in isolation listening only to loyalists. One of the great failures in the Presidency is that it does not have the proper indicators and early warning system on domestic policy. A President too often does not know what is going on around the country. The bureaucracies do but they are large, cumbersome, and fragmented. The problem is: how do you pull them together? A Department of Agriculture cannot view the total needs of farmers any more, if it ever could. So how do you bring these components together in an interdisciplinary sense. The White House staff needs to concentrate on a planning function. Roosevelt made an attempt with the National Resources Planning Board, but it concentrated on the physical more than the social or programmatic aspects. Nixon tried it with a social indicator-goals approach, but that lapsed whereas it should be one of the continuing functions of a Chief Executive. Where are we going? What are the priorities? How do we get there? By what time? Once those decisions have been reached through a consultation process, the President, backed by a responsive staff apparatus, should lead the Cabinet and other principal officials in achieving such a program. Too frequently, as has been stated, Congress has delegated the statutory authority directly to the executive departments, rather than to the President. This is very different from the British cabinet system. And while I have written on the Cabinet and favored the idea of a question period where the executives of the Federal government would appear weekly before both houses of Congress to respond to questions posed by the majority and minority, I do not favor the British cabinet system, as such, being imposed in this country, because it is the President elected by all the people who has that responsibility.

I agree with Don Price, now Dean of the John F. Kennedy School at Harvard, who said during the Truman administration that a President needs to be able to ask anyone he pleases for advice; he needs to have his associates meet whenever he pleases; he needs to have them consider whatever topics he may assign and then after hearing their advice, it is he who must decide. Those proceedings must be confidential. Who should participate should be flexible rather than rigid.

As a Cabinet assistant during the Eisenhower administration, one of the principal advantages I saw in the regular, institutionalized use of the Cabinet was that it offered each of its members the opportunity to be a part of an Administration, not simply the representative of a department. When the Secretary of Labor travelled to Spokane and a question arose on foreign policy or agricultural or defense policy, he could respond as a member of that Administration and not as one who only saw the President twice in 15 months.

When you examine the role of will, and you recall what Mr. Hess suggested a President ought to do in a given time period, a good example of that is President Nixon's role in the establishment of revenue sharing. That is the type of significant change which a President ought to make and which will alter the course and evolution of American history. Indeed, I think when history views the Nixon administration, revenue sharing will be considered one of the most fundamental thrusts that any Administration has made.

As I look ahead to this last quarter century, I see an increasing need for crisis management and growing policy conflicts because of political party fragmentation. Because the people wish to pick and choose among individuals and personalities rather than between parties and particular issues, it will be difficult for any President to secure a mandate. I suspect we are in for a period of conflict and crisis management. I can only hope that the solutions come not from the ad-hocracy of a Kennedy-type administration but more from an institutionalization of process as reflected during the Eisenhower administration.

10

Political Limitations of Presidential Leadership

Thomas Cronin

Presidents are piecemeal programmers at best, they rarely engage in policy-making if you define policy-making as examining the relationship of one subject area to another and really thinking out the long-term consequences. Such rational policy-making rarely exists in the White House and what policy-making does result is almost always ad hoc, sort of an adhocracy of reaction to fires in the in-basket, not management by objectives but management by crisis which generally characterizes the Presidents of the past several Administrations.

Many of the themes discussed at this Symposium remind me of a statement made by John F. Kennedy when he was President; he said, "I used to wonder when I was a member of the House up on Capitol Hill how President Truman who was then in the White House could get into so much trouble. Now that I've been in the White House for a year, I'm beginning to get the idea, it's not very difficult." And I think much of what has gone on in the past couple of days has suggested some of the reasons, some of the rather deep institutional and personal reasons, why the Presidency is a troubled institution, and why it is that we're so often disappointed by the leadership we get or the leadership we don't get. And at this particular season, in an election year, there is a great deal of skepticism about whether anyone is available in either party who is qualified to be President. Art Buchwald summed it up perhaps for the Democrats when he said that they are well endowed with 18 candidates for Vice President. I happen to feel that the Office of the Vice Presidency ought to be abolished so I'm not sure what that particular statement really amounts to.

There is a lot of cynicism about whether the job of President is too big for anyone or whether the institution needs major reform. I have found people who are uninterested, as was suggested by Mr. Reedy and others. People feel that perhaps there is no one, and if you go out into the supermarkets of America and ask who is qualified or who do you favor, there's a lot of yawning going on which leads some people to believe it is a self-fulfilling prophecy of cyncism built up in America toward the office of the President. It reminds me a little bit of Ogden Nash's statement in the form of a four-line poem, which goes as follows:

> They of such refined and delicate palates
> That they can discover no one worthy of their ballots
> And then, when someone terrible gets elected
> They say, there, that's just what I expected.

And I think there's some of that at work this year.

Another thing that sort of amuses me this year is that we tend to glorify and congratulate the candidate who drops out of the race, like Senator Walter Mondale, and we tend to disparage and deprecate the candidates who get in and as soon as they get in they're labeled as a politician, a lot of cynicism develops, and why are they running and they're not qualified. I'm an acquaintance of Sargent Shriver and he's one of the victims of this type of discussion. I had a discussion with one of his sons, Anthony Shriver, last summer when Sargent was deciding whether to run. In 1972 Anthony Shriver was in the fourth grade and, following the defeat of Geroge McGovern and his father in the 1972 election, Anthony was in class a week later and some kids came up to him, one kid in particular, and said, "Ha, ha, your daddy lost the election." Anthony really didn't know what to say. I think quite correctly he said, "Ha, ha, your daddy didn't even run.'' There really is something to that. I think we've got to reassess our attitudes and skepticism toward politics. Plato was right, what is honored in the country will be cultivated there, and we are not honoring or cultivating the best of the political class in America. And cynicism and the denigration of politics and politicians which grew up in the past decade are not highly novel, but the disillusionment with politics has tremendously increased in the Watergate period and has to be reversed; I think as Americans all of us have got to work very hard to do that.

PRESIDENTIAL PARADOXES

On the paradoxes of the institution of the Presidency, I think at the heart of the matter is the fact that we as a society simultaneously expecting Presidents to do two different types of performances, thus creating a no-win kind of job. Take Mr. Ford's case; we were very pleased at the outset that we had a common man, an average down-to-earth, non-imperial President for awhile, until people decided that not only did they want a common man, but they also wanted an uncommon performance. That's one of the paradoxes, and I'd like to tick off about a half dozen others in which we really want two different types of things. Not all of them are necessarily mutually exculsive but often they are. For example, this very one, we want a common person in many respects, someone who is representative of the country, who is not going to be aloof and arrogant or isolated from the average people of America, and yet it is abundantly clear that we also want an uncommon performance, someone who in addition to traits of commonness is also a gifted organizer, a gifted leader, a decisive, brilliant organizer of their staffs and cabinets and who can attract the best advisers in the country and knows how to use those advisers well. So we want uncommon performance, yet we want the sort of common sense of the common man in America.

The second paradox is that we want a decent and just person, a humane and gentle person, and yet I think Americans also want a ruthless and tough person with almost a touch of larceny in his heart. Can he make the tough decisions and will he be decisive, strong, and forceful? Often times toughness vies with another cherished commodity—decency and sense-of-gentleness justice. Frequently it is said that Adlai Stevenson was too nice a person, as if to say that if someone was too nice he wouldn't make a good President. And this is an interesting dichotomy—decency versus almost a touch of ruthlessness. It was an attractive quality in Robert Kennedy's campaign that he had this label of ruthless; actually it attracted, it looked like what we needed. I think we want both and that poses a problem. We want our President to be the national unifier; we also want the President to be the national divider in a sense of being a priority center and party leader.

It's necessarily in the job description of the Presidency that he has to be a national divider and here Presidents are caught coming and going. We want our President to be the head of state, a symbolic leader to accentuate what is common and accentuate the positive aspects of America; these are unifying types of functions and roles. But there's so much of the job as budget setter, as coalition builder, as party leader, that requires the President necessarily to be decisive and to counteract or countervail the unifying role. We want a President who is above politics and yet the job of the Presidency is intricately and ultimately a very political job. Nearly everything a President does has political overtones to it and yet there's a strong notion that the President should somehow be above politics, and somehow as soon as he becomes President forego a lifelong tradition of having been in politics, which is an impossibility. The Presidency is necessarily a highly political job. We cannot take the President out of politics and it would be undesirable anyway. Many ideas such as a six-year Presidential term with reelection forbidden implicitly contain the notion that somehow the Presidency could be freed from politics that way; it is not so. It would be an extremely political job in any event regardless of its term, and it is naive to think that we can remove the Presidency from politics.

We define politics frequently as a scheming, intriguing sort of selfishness by people in office, but there is a more positive definition of politics I think we ought also to consider. A positive definition of politics is that it is the art of making the difficult and desirable possible. And it necessarily involves negotiation, compromise, bargaining, and skilled political coalition-building.

Certain paradoxes result from the political prerequisites of the Presidential job. One is that what is needed to win the office often times is not the same thing as that which is required to be President or to govern the nation. I think David Broder has very nicely pointed to this particular problem when he said, "People who win primaries may become good Presidents, but it ain't necessarily so." Organizing well is important in governing just as it is in winning primaries, but the Nixon years should teach us that good advance men do not necessarily make trustworthy White House aides. Running the national government is a little more complicated than making the motorcade run on time. Many of the promises and many of the necessities of campaigning for the Office also run counter to what a President has to do to govern in the White House. For example, Douglass Cater suggests that it is important to reorganize the Cabinet but what happens during political campaigns for the Presidency limits the opportunity for such rational planning. At campaign time Presidential candidates are frequently tempted to promise more and more Cabinet and departmental offices to various interest groups, which runs counter to what President Nixon, for example, was quite rightly trying to do in trying to consolidate the Cabinet into more general multipurpose, general-interest departments on the domestic side of the Executive Branch.

The last paradox to which I want to refer is, that the job of the Presidency is necessarily an on-the-job learning experience, and yet we are dissatisfied with this. We don't like a president to have to engage in a great deal of on-the-job learning. We would like that to occur beforehand but the difficulty is there is really no job or experience prior to becoming President that really is a true preparation for being President. There is no apprenticeship; certainly the Vice Presidency is not a proper apprenticeship for the job of the President.

LACK OF LONG-RANGE PLANNING

We really don't achieve much long-range planning in the Presidency. There is a great deal of thought and discussion now developing about the fact that we need to have long-range Presidential planning. Senator Humphrey has argued for and introduced a bill last year with Senator Javits for a planning board in the White House and for planning processes and mechanisms. I think that we need to give a great deal more consideration to not only whether such planning will work but also where it should be located, if it should indeed be located in Washington. The facts of the matter are that Presidents are piecemeal programmers at best; they rarely engage in policymaking. If you define policymaking as looking at the relationships of one area to another and really thinking out the long-term consequences, rarely do we see policymaking or vigorous long-term thinking. It rarely exists in the White House. I'd like to suggest a number of reasons why we rarely get such policymaking and why policymaking is almost always a sort of adhocery or reaction to fires in the inbasket. It is not management by objective but management by crises which generally has characterized the Presidents of the past several administrations.

The first reason concerns the electoral connection—that elections are rarely our finest hour and are not adult education programs which really revolve around the issues. One is reminded of Earl Long in Louisiana. One time he ran for a year and a half to be elected Governor of Louisiana, and when he got into the governor's mansion the first thing he did after having campaigned for a year and a half against raising taxes was to call for all sorts of new taxes. His campaigners advised that he couldn't do this. Earl Long looked them in the eye and said, "I lied." We find time and again that during campaign times what candidates speak out on and promise does not really come about. President Nixon promised an open Presidency in the 1968 campaign and as you may recall, in fact, most candidates for office with rare exceptions do make things not perfectly clear. They try desperately to make things perfectly opaque and the idea of having a secret plan or being vague about matters generally is the case with rare exceptions like Barry Goldwater's. His motto was we'll give you a choice not an echo. Regular members of the Republican party, however, responded that they wanted a chance not a choice, and I think that illustrates the struggle. There's a tendency therefore to avoid; it's a fight to get elected, not a fight to educate and to plan for the future during election season. We will be frustrated this year, as we always are in quadrennial elections, because of this electoral connection and the effect that it has on the Presidency.

The second reason is that politicians have a lifelong instinct and yearning for flexibility. They are suspicious of being in advance of their time. A definition of a politician concerned with pluralities and majorities is that necessarily he or she is very suspicious of being in advance of their time. Leave my options open is what LBJ used to say. The politician's views insofar as they are distinguishable must be endlessly reversible said Garry Wills, and I think he has an overstated but valid point. The urgency imperative is another factor. The urgency factor—don't just stand there, do something—becomes imperative for Presidents even though they may not know what they are doing. The implicit motto of the Johnson White House was, Pass now, plan later. We'll make it work in the second term; we'll try to make it work after it's on the books. I didn't get elected to study things is what democratic activists frequently will say. I got elected to do things. It is imperative to try to fix things, solve problems, rather rapidly.

Another reason why Presidents do not engage in long-range planning is the knowledge problem. We often really don't have the knowledge about what a model city is, about what a good education is. Theodore White in the mid-1960's said in a Life magazine cover story, "Never have ideas been sought more hungrily nor tested against reality more quickly. From White House to City Hall scholars stalk the corridors of American power." The fact of the matter is the best and the brightest who took part in domestic, foreign policy, and economic issues were not able really to engage in much other than ad hoc planning and management by crises, and we were not able to look ahead. I think the fact is that advisers were way over their heads time and again, offering advice on matters about which we knew very little. I have run into a few people recently who will not at least in the privacy of their homes or studies concede that during the 1950's and 1960's academics and so-called expert advisers were giving and demanding the right to give advice as giants when they were still pygmies. We didn't have then and we still don't have now more than a very small amount of knowledge when it comes to the problems of recession and inflation, urban social problems, the behavior of electorates, and scores of other exceedingly complex matters in which so many of us were really willing or eager to give profusely of our counsel. There has been a loss of innocence I think with respect to this. There is now a great deal of feeling that we need to learn a great deal more about the consequences and the ramifications of social policy, of governmental intervention policy in the economy, and so on before we do things with confidence.

There are two other factors; one is the wanting to do everything at once problem. President Johnson with whom I worked for awhile often wanted to make every major problem that came to his attention the number one priority of the nation. The problem is if you make everything the number one priority of the nation, then nothing is the number one priority and you really have lost your whole ethic of setting priorities and trying to mobilize and build coalitions around that which is needed. This is a problem, trying to do many things as against very few. It is a problem the political class frequently confronts.

The last problem is that long-range planning is hard to do and politically dangerous. The difficulty with national goals and long-range social indicators is that they too quickly become standards by which to judge not the future but the present. In a sense, they institutionalize the creation of discontent. Once goals are established by a White House or by a President and it is agreed upon by everyone that the future will have to be very different from the present, it becomes absurd to be content with the present. The most extraordinary progress counts for little if it takes society only to a middle point on a uncompleted journey.

One last suggestion I would have is to agree very strongly with some of the thoughts expressed in the Stephen Hess paper. The limits of the Presidency are enormous and if we impose on it both grieviously high expectations on the one hand and also more and more responsibility such as the major role for planning in America on the other, we will no doubt be engaged in an act of weakening the Presidency rather than strengthening it. We've got to be very careful not to have a dependency complex where we ask our Presidents to do far more than they're able to do. We've got to look elsewhere in the system, elsewhere in the public sector and the private sector, multiple centers of leadership, multiple centers in which bright policy analysis can take place, in which forward thinking and at least a semblance of planning can take place.

QUESTION AND ANSWER

QUESTION: I wanted to speak to Dr. Cronin's remarks and ask for a comment. There was an article by Harry Wilson, I think, a very damning article about politicians in which it was argued that they have to be basically shysters and compromisers and sort of the lowest level of humanity in order to get elected and stay elected. And I wonder if you could comment on this?

DR. CRONIN: That's right; in the October 1975 *Harper's Magazine* Harry Wilson wrote an article that was very damning. His essential point was that the high ego problems and mediocrity in politicians that we generally take as vices are in his judgment actually virtues, that the politician who doesn't have a high ego and isn't mediocre is actually dangerous. It was, I think, an overstated article. The politician comes in as the butt of a great deal of humor in America. There are several definitions of a politician that take us in that direction, and I might offer a couple of them before I speak to your question. One that I have come across recently says that politicians take money from the rich and votes from the poor and the promise of protecting each from the other. Frank Kent who used to write for the *Baltimore Sun* once said that the able political campaigner is one who says something to everyone while at the same time saying nothing against anyone. Which reminds me of the young fellow running for Congress in 1974 who was caught saying, "I promise, if elected, to be neither partial nor impartial." If you say that quickly and move on to your next argument, it sounds very statesmanlike. The fact is that there are many incentives during a campaign for a politician to be glib, to not really speak about issues, and to—in our winner-take-all system—to build a coalition. A great number of candidates would like to speak about issues, would like to be smoked out. It's a great responsibility to the public during election time to smoke out the candidates, to ask Presidential candidates who are promising things exactly what they would do and how they would do it if elected.

We have a lot of cheap talk from almost all the candidates right now about how big bureaucracies and big Washington government are horrible, and how if they get elected they'll dismantle them or do something to them. Very few candidates, however, have really been taken to task and asked what is it that you would do to make the Executive Branch of the government responsive, what would you do to make an open Presidency? Candidate Nixon in 1968 promised us an open Presidency but no one really bothered to ask him what he meant by this, what would he actually do. It wound up that he didn't have the foggiest idea of what an open Presidency was and we simply didn't get one, did we? But I think the responsibility is ours, not the candidates'. The incentive to them is to be vague and to collect as many votes as possible; the responsibility of the citizens is to ask them to explain as much as possible, to try to pin them down. Will they hold regular press conferences in the White House? Will they use the Cabinet intelligently? Will they be willing occasionally to say that they've made mistakes?

Too often being President means you never have to say you're sorry. Or being President means never having to say you were wrong. Or being President means never having to say you don't have all the answers. The fact of the matter is our Presidents are put into a bind whereby we do not allow them to come forward and say they are confused, they do not know what's going on, and they need help, and there's all sorts of conflicts in their own Executive Office and their own Cabinet. The firing of James Schlesinger is a good case in point. Ford was not allowed to say to the American public that his Cabinet members disagree. He was not allowed to say, for example, that he was going to hold an hour-long meeting in the East Room and he would like to have the networks come in and televise it and he would like Kissinger and Schlesinger to discuss how they differ and his own view was to side with Kissinger but he respected Schlesinger very much as he was a very able Secretary of Defense. We don't allow that, as if they have a unified voice and a unified view when in fact matters are far more complex.

So I think the burden of changing the attitude and the system toward politicians is largely one that we've got to look at, particularly political science teachers in college and secondary schools. If we understood better the incentive system that shapes the performance of politicians, and the complexity of issues, then I think we might be able to reverse this unnecessary burden of cynicism about politicians.

11

Planning and the Presidency

Douglass Cater

Responding to the political exigencies of the moment does not produce the long-range planning needed in the White House. The kind of leadership we need in the Presidency can emerge from institutionalized mechanisms such as the Council of Economic Advisors and the annual report it produces, "centers of organized intelligence" to define long-term policy options, and a leader in office who is prepared to redefine the job of the Presidency.

We have surveyed the forces which play on the President. My assignment is to examine one additional force: the force of the future. We are told that Presidents play for the future; among their chief aims is to achieve a place in the history books. But the question should be asked, How does the future play on the President? I submit a tentative answer—not very well.

Let us suppose that a President learns of some event, years distant, which would be catastrophic in impact but would require great social cost and political effort to head off. Would he or wouldn't he? This is not entirely speculative. This past year scientists have been considering tentative findings that not only hair sprays and supersonic aircraft may be affecting the ozone layer of our atmosphere but also nitrogen fertilizer, the basic means of sustaining the high yield of our farms here and around the world, may be causing damage that could have serious consequences by the end of the century. There are other issues—issues of energy, of environment, of pollution, issues on the scientific frontiers such as genetic manipulation—which may have to engage Presidential leadership. These are quiet but deadly crises that do not come to a sudden head so that crisis management can take over—crises that require long-range anticipation, intensive and cross-disciplinary planning, and the capacity to maintain a policy over a sustained period of time.

I differ somewhat with the perspectives of Messrs. Hess and Horn that a President can divide and delegate his job among his Cabinet members. The societal issues with which a President is going to be grappling the rest of this century seldom fall into the neat categories of the existing government departments. The Cabinet officer presides over a particular empire and becomes jealous in preserving its territory. It has not been by happenstance or by egomania alone that our recent Presidents have downgraded their Cabinets. The important question is how to reorganize the business of government so that the subdivisions of the Cabinet are more relevant to the urgent business of the Presidency.

RESTRICTED PLANNING

Why is it so difficult for a President to deal with the long run? I went to the White House as a journalist who thought he had been rather close to the business of the Presidency. I was totally unsettled by the momentum of the White House, with the constant incessancies driving the President and those immediately around him. The preoccupation with the hurry-up-and-do-it-now becomes the dominant mood of a dynamic President.

One story will illustrate this. In 1965, after talking to a number of people in the health field, I submitted a memorandum to President Johnson urging that he bring the leading experts together to define long-range health goals for America. I submitted that memorandum at ten o'clock one night. The next morning at 6:30 the phone by my bed was ringing. It was the President. He was going out to give a speech later that morning and requested, "Can't we have about three or four of those health goals to put into my speech?"

The President is working with deadlines that are as regular and urgent as those of the average reporter. Johnson had a very profound, if not particularly eloquent approach to the business of dealing with Congress. He would say, "If you're not doing it to them, they're doing it to you." Sometimes he substituted other words for "it." He was preoccupied with the limited run of a Presidential mandate. The power a President gets at the time of election is a depletable resource. It has to be used swiftly if it's going to be used fruitfully. The result in the Johnson White House was a continual race for program. In 1964 a series of task forces had been set up which reported the week after the election so that the agenda for the next year's program could be put together in time to go to Congress in January. This became an annual routine which worked pretty well considering that this was a breakthrough period after a prolonged time of stalemate. Each spring the President's assistants would fly all over the country to small meetings to canvass what Johnson called "the best ideas" about what needed to be done. Out of the gleanings of those flights came the summer task forces and by autumn there would be the screening by the professional agencies of the government. This led to a Christmas shopping list for the President so that his program could be unveiled each January.

This was about as far as forward planning went. We made the attempt to have five-year projections of dollar costs for each new program. But Congress learned about this and demanded details of these projections. The President concluded this would freeze his options and create added resistances.

Several forces work against long-range forward planning in the White House. One is the fear of an institutionalized bureaucracy which will serve as an additional burden. There is the fear of pressure groups that could be stirred up if a President attempts to look beyond the immediate. There is the concern that a strong President must be the constant innovator and each year must come up with new ideas, or at least old ideas newly packaged.

But what of the future President? Mr. Hess has described the Ultimate Modern Presidency in his paper; I find this a very interesting concept. Is this UMP going to be able to live by the LBJ model? I would suggest that the answer is no. We have heard repeatedly in this Symposium that the Ultimate Modern President must be more honest, more open, and less manipulative. He will be obliged to go contrary to all the traditions of salesmanship in America. The Ultimate Modern President has got to be more participatory. He must let not only Congress but also the people in on the act at earlier stages. He will be dealing with a slower growth economy so that he will not have the incremental revenues that permit a dynamic President to take new initiatives. The Ultimate Modern President is going to have to deal with more distant problems if he intends to be relevant to the challenges of the late twentieth century.

APPROACHES TO LEADERSHIP

How do we get that kind of leadership? I would suggest briefly three approaches. First, we need to look to the mechanisms within the Presidency which will encourage his distant visions of the nation and its needs. The model of the Council of Economic Advisors and of the President's obligation to make an annual economic report represents a beginning. We all know that economic indicators alone are not adequate to measure where we are and where we wish to go in society. We need social indicators for which social science is ill prepared. There need to be other perspectives for a President's vision besides the gross national product (GNP) and the rate of employment.

Second, we need institutions outside the Presidency—what Walter Lippman called "centers of organized intelligence"— which help define long-term policy options for the country. Here, too, we are still in a primitive stage in providing meaningful intelligence for a President's agenda.

Third, we need a President who is willing to redefine the job of the Presidency. The Ultimate Modern President must be a person who looks beyond the traditional hats in his or her haberdashery.

I differ with my friend and colleague George Ready about the role of the public as we wait for the Ultimate Modern President. Reedy pointed to the periods of 1850-1860 and 1920-1932, suggesting that we might presently be in the same trough in which leadership is literally impossible. Yet when we examine those earlier periods, it took a Lincoln and a Roosevelt to signal that a new era had begun. We must continue to make the search for a leader to help us out of the present trough. It is not your job or my job to sit back passively and wait for this leader to emerge.

One perspective I have from having served five years in the White House is of the human frailty of the individual who holds the Presidency. No matter how hard he seeks the office, until he gets there he know very little about the nature of that job. We are fortunate when he proves to be a person with quick perceptions and a capacity for on-the-job training. Remember that Franklin Roosevelt ran on a campaign of cutting the budget to make ends meet. Most of our Presidents have been men who had few ideas in advance about what they wanted to do.

Here is where we come in. We help define the job and we help shape the person who emerges in the job. This constitutes our challenge and our immediate task.

QUESTION AND ANSWER

QUESTION: Is it possible that there has been not a little but too much planning, perhaps an excess of planning in the wrong direction?

MR. CATER: Planning can be grossly faulted. But our task is to find ways to improve it or else to accept the consequences and conclude that we can go back to non-planning in America. It seems to me that we do have certain models—the Council of Economic Advisors has changed the climate of decision-making from a time when there was no basic knowledge on which the economic decisions of government could be made. Admittedly, given the experience of the last three or four years, we've had a reduction of faith in the annual economic report which is reviewed by Congress and which forces aggregate thinking about economic policy. I would think that the experience since the passage of the Employment Act of 1946 has given us certain guidelines about what you can do and what you can't do. Public opinion has concluded that the economic indices of a society should not be the total measure for future planning. What is there beyond that? This is the question I'm raising.

COMMENTARY

AARON WILDAVSKY: The remarks by Doug Cater and Tom Cronin and the fact that I can hardly be held responsible for 10 minutes of commentary off the cuff lead me to try to put in some perspective our feelings of dissatisfaction about the Presidency and about planning and the future. I think now these things can in fact be related so that instead of becoming really disparate statements, like beads on a string, we can see some relationship among them.

What has happened, I think, is that we want President Ford to take seriously the future consequences of present domestic activity and we want him not to consider at all the future consequences of present foreign activity. And it is these opposed feelings that lend the order of inconsistency to our demands and his responses. Think of faith—faith is the willingness to act in the absence of things seen. In foreign policy, we have no faith. We have to wait until the consequences of events are upon us so, like a doubting Thomas, a Congressional delegation will go to Cambodia and put its hands in the wound of the people, pick up its fingers, and say, Yes, there's blood.

Consider what's going on in Angola. The President says there will be terrible future consequences of this. The country says, Says you, we don't believe this. And he says, You're only thinking of the present but if the Soviets and Cubans establish a foothold, right, and then Soviets establish naval bases and air bases and this will link up with Somaliland, and Somaliland like the knee bone and the thigh bone is going to link up with the Middle East and then 20 years from now there will be terrible consequences. We hear no liberal planners saying, Wonderful, you are taking into account the future. Hell, no, because there's no belief and there's no faith. We say, Show us and that means afterwards. My own view is that the President greatly erred, led by the Secretary of State, because he tried to deal with foreign policy like it was foreign policy instead of like it was domestic policy, which it is because when there's no faith it's all domestic policy. He has to use it as a learning experience. If the bad things come, then maybe in the future people will see that there's some point in considering the future. But as it is, the events that we have seen are totally predictable. The Secretary of State, in his usual aggrieved way, expects support when not one person in this audience would believe he would get support in Angola; then he says, Isn't it terrible there is no support for foreign policy in this country? We must be in a terrible period of decline and yes, indeed, action becomes abortion as we cut them off in Angola.

In regard to Vietnam or into other foreign policy questions all the presidential comments are indeed forward planning. What of the domino theory? What are all these other theories but theories of contingencies, lasting long into the future, one depending on another? But when it comes to domestic policy, the President, being conservative, doesn't want to consider the possible tangential conceivable future consequences of everything because that means you'd have to have vast governmental control; stop this, don't do that, don't breathe, don't smoke, God knows what you couldn't do. The only area in which he thinks of the future, of course, is government spending, which is bad.

I read a paper not long ago on a medical syndrome in which the organism dies because an infection triggers off every single defense mechanism it has. That is, it's not the initial disease, but the fact that in an effort to protect itself against every conceivable eventuality everything starts flowing at once, the individual overconsumes internal energy. If you start thinking of all the cassandras we have on the things that are bad for you to eat, and the things that are bad for you to smell, and the things that are bad for you to breathe, and the things that are happening underground and overground and in interplanetary space, you begin to understand that if we were to take action, not in the presence of evidence, because it's always in dispute, but on the basis of what some people think we shouldn't be doing, we could probably consume the entire gross national product and go poof. I point out to you a simple thing; I happen to like Fresca, that is I used to like Fresca when it had cyclamates and then some idiots decided that if you ate 17 tons of Fresca you would get cancer. And now it appears, number one, that there's nothing wrong with cyclamates and, number two, that saccharin and other things may be marginally worse for us than the other things we were drinking. In our time we want the President to plan domestically, that is, to stop doing all these things that some group of society thinks is terrible but nobody wants him to plan foreign policy because they don't have trust in what he will do.

As for planning itself, I think we can stop tons of controversy by understanding that planning is the capacity to act in the present to control the future. Therefore, if you succeed in planning you're perfect. So if once you put in your mind planning equals perfection then you understand that planning is the word for all those things we would like to have in the future that we don't know how to get. Therefore, when people say we should plan more, they're really saying we should be more perfect and we should do better. But they don't really mean, that we should act now, when if we waited a few years we would have much better information to act on most future decisions. They can't really mean that, or do they mean we understand how to map out the whole future for everybody and we ought to impose it on them?

Let's consider here what a little bit of public policy analysis can tell us. The most important thing to understand about health policy, going to Mr. Cater's idea of goals, is there is no connection between medicine and health beyond a minimal amount. How healthy you are depends on what your mother always told you, how to live, not on how often you go to the doctors. How healthy people are depends on such things as eating a good breakfast, sleeping 7 or 8 hours a day, not 4 or 14 hours a day; if you want to be healthy, don't drink, don't smoke, don't eat too much, don't be nervous. How could being healthy depend on hospitals? It's true that if you have a broken leg or some disease for which medicine is useful it's very good to have a doctor, but when there are too many of them they start cutting too much, start prescribing too much. You hear, Let's plan now so we can improve the delivery of medical care services. Sometimes I think people are thinking like the Welcome Wagon Lady is coming, only she's a Health Wagon Lady and she has a package and she delivers health care to you. Now if it's a shot you can give people that lasts for five years, maybe we'll get hold of everybody in the country once, but if you understand that health delivery deals with such tangential aspects of human behavior, trivial things really, not worth discussing, like what you eat, how long you sleep, whether and what you drink, whether you smoke, your psychological or psychic status, you understand that to deliver health requires massive, powerful, detailed intervention in human life in which that horrible buzzing in the car with the seat belt would be only the harbinger of things to come.

Let's take another brief crack at it in a different way. Let me give you a rule that you can follow here. Every socially desired indicator can be achieved without question, I guarantee you, so long as you don't care about what happens to any other. For example, I'll give you my fool-proof method for ending dope addiction in this country, which has in fact been tried in China and Japan, especially in China. The first time a person is caught with this stuff and you have random checks, urinalysis and so on, it's very easy to do, they're given a warning. The second time they are shot. You explain to them that they are imposing externalities on the rest of the population that cannot be borne and the cost of engaging in this pleasurable activity turns out to be greater than the pleasure and it stops. That is, if you don't care about life and liberty, it's easy. So, too, I can stop crime with very similar measures if I don't care about life, liberty, due process, decency, and all the rest of it. Therefore, when people are talking about an increase in social indicators and planning, they are simply encapsulated, in a different vocabulary, in unresolved conflict.

Let me give you two examples. One is oil policy. Probably the most important thing we could do to help most poor people in the world, to help most poor Americans, to reduce American domestic conflict, to make it hard on our enemies, to make it good for our allies, would be to reduce the price of oil. But you see what happened domestically; we can't drill offshore because oil might spill and that would be very bad for the birds. Obviously we cannot mine coal underground; it's very bad for the lungs. We cannot mine coal above it, strip mining, because that rips up the land. So that basically what we are saying is that it's a terrible crisis but we must absolutely not do any single thing about it. Then somebody says how about nuclear power plants. Oh, that's very bad, they could blow up. Right?

So you see that what can happen is that the consequences of trying to protect against everything can mean utter stultification. From the point of view of the Presidency, the President when he's urged to plan is really urged to make things come out better, but if we ourselves are inconsistent in the demands we make on Presidents—don't plan foreign policy, plan everything in domestic policy—we must not be surprised if they appear confused. I am here, of course, with the same message that Governor Brown, in his own way, has been trying to tell you, that is until we resolve what's in us, he will not be able to resolve what's in him. In any event, the one thing we should have learned by these past events is that Presidents certainly cannot make us happy, governments cannot make us happy, policies cannot make us happy but that doesn't mean they can't give us a lot of fun.

12

The Crisis
of the Presidency

Hubert H. Humphrey

The answer to abuses of authority committed by recent Presidents lies not in weakening the Presidency but in choosing individuals for the Office who can be trusted with its vast powers, trusted to use them fully and consistently with the letter and spirit of the Constitution. Such a President would combine the qualities of openness and strong political leadership. The recent crisis of the Presidency coincides with the crisis of confidence in our political parties and one cannot be restored without the other.

We meet for these discussions of the Presidency at a dark and confusing hour. In this the year of our Bicentennial celebration we are proud of our nation's achievements. The United States is not only the most powerful nation on earth. It is also—and far more importantly—the most durable republic in human history. We live under the oldest surviving written Constitution in the world.

Yet despite these very real achievements, we are in no mood for self congratulation. Too many of our people are out of work. Too many are hungry and inadequately housed. Too many of our cities and states are near default. And, worst of all, public confidence in our political institutions is at low ebb.

The truth is that this public doubt seems well deserved. The list of problems on the public agenda is long and frightening, but our government is deadlocked, at times almost paralyzed.

The President offers little leadership, and responds to Congressional efforts with a rain of vetoes. Without the cooperation of the executive branch, Congress has been hard pressed to develop a program for the nation.

Our government is simply not working properly, and people are beginning to wonder whether it is possible to summon up the will and strength to make it effective once again.

A generation of young people is growing up in an environment of political cynicism and alienation.

The Constitution has stood the test of time, and it is surely capable of adapting to the present crisis. The problem is not in our institutions. It is ourselves. Like the mythical Pogo, we "have met the enemy and they is us."

The beginning of the way out of our current predicament is the realization that it centers on the crisis of the Presidency. That is why discussions of the Presidency inevitably raise questions about the health of the whole system.

The Presidency, for better and for worse, in good times and bad, has become in Woodrow Wilson's phrase, "the vital place of action in the system." When that office is abused, or left dormant, the system's very life is threatened.

Originally the Framers intended that the powers of government be centered in Congress, the lawmaking body. The President's powers were outlined in almost cryptic terms, in a brief second article of the Constitution. They centered on his primary responsibility for the conduct of foreign relations, as commander-in-chief of the armed forces, and for the "faithful execution" of laws made by Congress.

There was some mingling of powers. The President could veto legislation. He was directed to report to Congress on "the state of the union" and to recommend measures that he deemed "Necessary and expedient."

Congress, in turn, had power to deny confirmation to executive appointments, and to withhold appropriations. But the basic division of labor seemed clear enough. Congress, the law-maker, was the primary policy-maker. The President was to administer the laws fairly and justly, and in the case of war to be the commander-in-chief, and to conduct foreign relations.

PRESIDENTIAL ENLARGEMENT

But the genius of the system, the quality that has enabled it to endure almost 200 years, is its flexibility and adaptability. The major adjustment, the one that has enabled the Constitution to adapt to modern times, has come with the "enlargement of the Presidency," in Rexford Tugwell's graphic phrase.

The phenomenon has not been confined to the United States. Throughout the western world, chief executives are no longer simply administrators of laws adopted by legislatures. The increasing interdependency of nations, and the increasing complexity of social and economic systems, has made expectation to fall on chief executives.

In our system, Congress still makes the laws, and the United States is still fundamentally a nation of law. In fact, the United States Congress is the most creative, most energetic legislature in the developed world, far more effective and independent than the legislative bodies in the great parliamentary democracies of Europe.

However, we live in an age in which positive government has become an inescapable necessity. And in an age of positive government, executive leadership—leadership that can comprehend the nation's situation as a whole, leadership that can develop a coherent vision of a better future, and then call the national community toward actions that bring that vision to reality—executive leadership of this kind has come to be expected, even demanded, by citizens of the leading democracy in the world. And the people are right.

Despite the changes wrought by the times, the system framed in the 18th century remains essentially intact. Power is still kept separated, shared among different authorities. It is still a fundamental principle of our system that no single person, no single group can be trusted with power alone.

This separation of power is a great blessing, as we have recently had opportunity to appreciate anew. For when a self-interested faction seizes control over one branch, another branch is there to restore discipline and fidelity to the system.

While there is good reason for keeping power separated, our system is also designed for cooperation and coordination between those separated branches, when the people give their confidence to a single party that is able to win the contest for the Presidency and hold control over both houses of Congress.

When this happens, the stage is set for a vigorous assault on the nation's problems—provided that the President can take the lead in presenting a strong legislative program and in marshalling the resources of the executive branch in the difficult day-to-day job of governing.

Such vigorous coordination has in fact taken place at crucial times in the Nation's history. It happened under Abraham Lincoln and the Republicans. The great advances of Theodore Roosevelt's New Nationalism and Woodrow Wilson's New Freedom, of Franklin Roosevelt's New Deal and Lyndon Johnson's Great Society likewise took place in moments of Constitutional coordination and Presidential initiative.

Some observers question whether the nation is ready now for a similar social and political renewal. After all, the pattern in our history has been for periods of Presidential enlargement to be succeeded by periods of pause and reaction.

Thus, after Andrew Jackson's vigorous leadership came the serious failures in leadership by Martin Van Buren and John Tyler. After James K. Polk's solid achievements, reactions set in during the Presidencies of Millard Fillmore, Franklin Pierce, and James Buchanan. Lincoln's boldness was followed by the impeachment of Andrew Johnson and the incompetence and scandals of the administration of Ulysses S. Grant. Woodrow Wilson's energetic efforts were followed by stagnation under Warren Harding and Calvin Coolidge.

Recalling this pattern, some observers conclude that we are in for a period of reaction to the so-called "imperial Presidency." Certainly we have witnessed gross abuses of Presidential power in recent years.

We have been lied to. The power of police agencies has been abused. Involvement in war, as in the civil war in Angola, and foreign intervention have been initiated without Congressional knowledge and approval. Funds for domestic programs have been impounded. Domestic agencies for economic development have been dismantled without Congressional approval. In short, we have lived in a period that has verged on Presidential autocracy.

It is understandable, in reaction to this pattern, that some people have wanted to weaken the office of the Presidency. But that response is undiscriminating and it is wrong.

The answer lies not in weakening the Presidency, but in choosing individuals for that office who can be trusted with its vast powers, trusted to use them in full and willing conformance with the letter and spirit of the constitutional provisions for sharing power. A Constitutional president must realize that his responsibility is not only to use the power vested in the Presidency, but to exercise self-discipline in its use.

And the answer lies in choosing individuals possessing imagination, courage, and self-discipline, so that the Presidency's vast powers are put to work in the people's behalf.

TWO CRITICAL ASPECTS

There are two critical aspects of the Presidency. The first is that it must be conducted openly, by political leaders who are not afraid to confide in the people. As Woodrow Wilson said, the President is "the political leader of the nation. . . .When he speaks in his true character, he speaks for no special interest. If he rightly interprets the national thought and boldly insists upon it, he is irresistible, and the country never feels the zest of action so much as when its President is of such insight and calibre."

In this spirit, if political battle must be waged, as often it must be, the President must be determined to enlist the people on his side. And he must do so openly and candidly, not by deception.

This openness is essential, but it is not enough. Recent events have seemed to offer the choice between a vigorous Presidency conducted behind closed doors, and an open Presidency that is virtually inert. But that is a false choice. A President must be open and confiding, but he must also be a strong political leader, capable of winning support from other political leaders and from the people.

A President cannot lead alone. He must have the willing cooperation of other political leaders. Our system will not work otherwise. It is sometimes said that James K. Polk was the last President to manage the executive branch all by himself. That is probably an exaggeration, but even so, remember that in 1848, when Polk was President, the federal budget was around 50 million dollars a year, and the civilian payroll was around 25 thousand employees, four-fifths of them in the postal service. Yet the job of managing a federal government even of this size completely exhausted Polk. He died a broken and bitter man, just a few months after leaving the White House.

If Polk was crushed by the labor of managing the federal government in 1848, it is obvious that the job can no longer be accomplished by direct command.

President Truman once remarked that General Eisenhower would have a hard time adjusting to the Presidential office given his military background. "The General will order 'Do this and do that.' And you know what?" Truman chuckled, "*Nothing will happen.*" For this was precisely the sad experience of another General-become-President, Ulysses Grant.

A President must lead by persuasion. And he must persuade, not just his own staff and people of his own appointment in the federal government, but independently elected public officials throughout the land. There is no other way that our Constitutional system can be made to work. The President must be a person who can win the willing cooperation of independent citizens.

THE GAINING OF CONSENT

The essence of democratic government does not lie in giving commands, but in gaining consent. The Presidency, said Teddy Roosevelt, "is a bully pulpit." Yes indeed, the President must be the moral leader of the nation. But he must be more than a political philosopher and evangelist. He must be the teacher, the persuader, the advocate, the healer, and the counselor.

Let me illustrate what I mean more concretely.

The Presidency, the vital center of our governmental system, is the link that binds the political branches of the federal government. The President's primary instrument in this task is his political party. It is no coincidence that the recent crisis of the Presidency has been matched by a crisis in the major political parties. One cannot be restored without the other.

Genuinely popular government demands effective political parties. If the President is to rally the people to common purpose, he must first rally his political party.

The great Presidents of both parties have recognized this responsibility, and eagerly met it. Thomas Jefferson, Andrew Jackson, Abraham Lincoln, Theodore Roosevelt, Woodrow Wilson, Franklin Roosevelt, and in our own time, Harry Truman, John Kennedy and Lyndon Johnson—all have stood forth as leaders of their parties.

The spectacle of the more recent past, by contrast, dramatically illustrates the need for Presidential leadership that does not shrink from the party connection, but rather leadership that is in a position to capitalize on it. Only through this leadership can legislation and administration be brought together behind a program to deal with the challenges facing the country.

Party leadership is one of the President's most difficult, most demanding tasks. American parties are notoriously undisciplined. They are not idealogically narrow or simple. American parties are broad, diverse, complex, and filled with internal tensions. One of the President's first responsibilities is to take the lead in finding common ground, on which all of his party's elements can stand, and to teach them the habit of standing together.

Broad as American parties are, they do present a real constituency for a President who can mobilize it. A President who intends to act positively, to lead the people in common enterprise for the public welfare, will find most of his natural allies gathered in the Democratic Party. If he can rally that party, he can build majorities for his program. The country has been without this kind of leadership for nearly a decade.

The importance of Presidential leadership for the party has been dramatically illustrated during the last session of Congress. In the Congressional elections of 1974, a large new group of Representatives was elected and came to Washington full of bright hopes for a more responsive and active government. Now after a year of dubious battle with a White House that has utterly failed to give clear direction, the "Class of 1974" is understandably discouraged.

A year ago, there was some talk among people who should know better that this Congress might be "veto proof." Now, a cruel disillusion has set in.

But the Congress ought not have to be "veto proof" to be effective. Our system was *not* designed for confrontation. It was designed for shared power and responsibility in a spirit of accommodation.

The system was designed for cooperation, in the public interest. The new young members of Congress, and many of their elders, have good legislative ideas. They are prepared with bills that address the problems of this nation. They have, in fact, accomplished a great deal. But the utter lack of executive cooperation—indeed, the prospect that these good ideas would be blocked by vetoes—has sacrificed much of the promise that existed just one year ago.

One of the most discouraging episodes in the last disheartening year was the recent struggle over the tax cut. Everyone agreed that the tax cut should be extended. Meanwhile, Congress was in the midst of implementing the new Budget Control Act, which requires Congressional discipline in relating revenues and expenditures. Many were skeptical about this Act when it was passed, but even the skeptics now admit that it is working remarkably well.

President Ford, however, refused to recognize this progress. Instead, he set himself against it, insisting that Congress tie a spending ceiling to the tax cut—a spending ceiling for the fiscal year beginning ten months from now. It was a foolish demand in any case, but particularly so in light of the progress that Congress has been making in disciplining itself on budgetary matters.

NATIONAL—STATE RELATIONS

The Presidency is a vital link in our political system in another sense, too. It is the link that binds the elements of the federal system together. Our national government spends billions of dollars each year on domestic purposes. We most urgently need a more effective way to administer these services. Part of the answer lies in a more creative use of the federal system.

Washington does not have all the answers. The time has come to recognize that there is solid experience and competence, as well as grass-roots knowledge, in our state capitals.

We know that government must be more responsive and efficient. One major step to achieve this is to establish a close relationship between the chief executives—between the President and the fifty state Governors.

In recent years, partly through revenue sharing and federal grants and loans, state governments have been growing in competence and importance. Also, because of the Supreme Court rule of one-man, one-vote, state legislatures have become much more representative and thereby more responsive to the needs of the people. State legislatures today are filled with young men and women of talent and competence, with imagination and ability. Also, the office of governor has been attracting able men and women, capable of administering complex affairs, and eager to understand the affairs of their states in a broader, regional framework.

We ought to encourage this important development. Governors should be drawn into closer coordination with one another, and with the federal government, through the establishment of regional Executive Councils, each one including a federal representative appointed by, and reporting directly to, the President.

These Regional Councils should be responsible for planning and administering federal programs in their area, on the basis of plans prepared by the Governors of each region, working in cooperation with regional representatives of the federal departments.

But something more is needed to make our federal system cooperative and efficient. Our country is characterized by cultural, geographic and economic differences. These differences can either add to our strength or be a serious problem in the conduct of government.

Therefore, I propose that the modern Presidency should include the establishment of a Federal Council, consisting of the 50 Governors and the President. This council should meet regularly on a systematic basis so that the President may outline to the Governors his proposals and initiatives, and receive from the Governors their advice and counsel in the preparation of the federal budget, the administration of the departments, and the implementation of federal laws.

There is no substitute for the personal working relationship between the President and the State executives. The federal system is not just the government in Washington. It is a national government represented by the President and the 50 State governments represented by the Governors.

BASIC CHALLENGES

We live in a time in which doubts about democracy are very profound. Everyone agrees that government of, by, and for the people is a great dream, but many doubt that it will work for a nation that spans a continent and includes regions of the utmost variety. Certainly, the administration of such a government requires better planning than we have had in this country until now.

Our forefathers struggled against tyranny, against government by birth, by wealth, or class, and against sectionalism. Today, we struggle against confusion, ineffectiveness, waste, bureaucracy, and inefficiency. Our struggle is less glorious than theirs, but just as critical, if the dream of democracy is to be realized. The search now must be for means of coordinating a more decentralized administration. That is one of our primary challenges.

Another basic challenge is for the United States to become a mature world power. We have become a world power but, regrettably, as a representative government we have only a half-world knowledge.

And this is understandable. As Adlai Stevenson once said, "Government is like a pump, and what it pumps up is just what we are—a fair sample of the intellect, the ethics, and the morals of the people, no better, no worse." And I might add that while power can come swiftly, knowledge and judgment come through long experience of pain, suffering, study, and action.

We must recognize the *limits* of power in this modern age—power that recognizes the rights and aspirations of other nations and people; and power that is used with resolution, when vital interests are genuinely at stake, but always with restraint. Above all, it will be power that is *shared* to promote the benefits of peace and development throughout the community of nations. And, it must be power that is exercised with a constant sense of moral obligation.

However, this mature understanding of the exercise of power by our nation, recognized as the greatest military and economic power in world history, must begin with a clear understanding of the limits and obligations of power in the Presidency itself, by the incumbent in that office.

The awesome power of the modern Presidency has tempted recent incumbents to dispense with the hard work of sharing their power. It has seemed too difficult, too risky, and unnecessary, at least in the short run, and especially in national security affairs, for the President to share his power with anyone who disagreed with him.

But we have learned that an autocratic Presidency is the greatest danger in our system. We need an *active* Presidency, but one moderated by the determination to take counsel widely. Our President must be a person to whom cooperation comes naturally, for whom coordination is a deeply ingrained habit and style of operation.

We expect our President to be active—to be a leader. But we must remember that the appropriate activity for a President is communication with the people, listening carefully to the voice of the land, and winning popular assent for good and necessary measures. He must not only lead the people, he must also heed their concerns. He must not only be the leader, but also the healer.

We are at the beginning of a critical election year. The leader chosen this year must rally the people to new effort. He must restore confidence in a system that has worked through storm and stress for 200 years, a system that has survived wars and depressions, but is now suffering an acute internal crisis.

No foreign foe, no economic crisis has been able to break the spirit of this nation. But leaders who broke faith with the people have tried its soul. Unless the confidence of the people is won back, the future is bleak. But if the energies of the people can be rallied, we will embark upon the third century with renewed confidence.

I do not accept the conventional assessment that Americans are ready to support a radical dismantling of governmental institutions and programs designed to achieve a higher level of justice and happiness among our citizens. That is not what people are saying when they tell public opinion experts about their disillusionment and cynicism.

No, the people are expressing their natural feelings toward a government that has failed to keep its promises and that has imposed sacrifices without accepting a corresponding obligation to deliver results.

The people are not necessarily asking for something new and

revolutionary. They are seeking a return to fundamentals, to standards that are basic and even old fashioned. People want honesty and integrity in public life. They want decency and fair play. They want to be trusted so that they can trust their government. They are seeking character and substance, rather than charisma and image.

The people are crying out for a government that *works* . . .one that understands their problems and that makes an honest and compassionate effort to help solve them. And when the people once again encounter such a government, they will give it their enthusiastic and loyal support.

Can a system based on free elections, or representation, on open decision-making, persist under modern conditions? The question is perpetual. The jury is out, as it always is. The record of the past inspires confidence. But a great deal depends upon the choice made this year, and on the quality of leadership provided by the person selected as the next President of the United States.

One of the great moral political leaders of our times was my dear and good friend, Adlai Stevenson. Adlai reminded us of the requirements of self-government, in a statement that reads as follows:

"Democracy is not self-executing. We have to make it work, and to make it work we have to understand it. Sober thought and fearless criticism are impossible without critical thinkers and thinking critics. Such persons must be given the opportunity to come together, to see new facts in the light of old principles, and evaluate old principles in the light of new facts, by deliberation, debate, and dialogue. This, as we all know well, though some of us forget from time to time, requires intellectual independence, impenitent speculation, and freedom from political pressure. For, democracy's need for wisdom will remain as perennial as its need for liberty; not only external vigilance, but unending self-examination must be the perennial price of liberty because the work of self-government never ceases."

QUESTION AND ANSWER

QUESTION BY MERVIN FIELD: I've listened to your speeches and your messages all my life and I've spent 5/6 of the time you have on this planet, and in a dispassionate way I would say that what you have said today was very powerful, very moving, very inspiring. If I were to really forget about where I was, I could visualize your saying for the reasons that I have just enunciated "I have decided that I will be a candidate for President of the United States." And I am mindful of what you said you were, I have heard you and I know your position that you do not want to announce your candidacy, that you will be available if the convention should come to you. And I understand your reservations about entering the primary system but suppose in the course of the next couple of months, and if this is not a fair question, don't answer it, because I don't want in this setting to ask an unfair question, but suppose that the situation developed where the public might misinterpret your very healthy and honest reservations about going into primaries and where they might interpret it as your failure to go into the primaries as some deficiency, as some unfair tactic on your part, they recognize that you really would like to be President, you've stated yourself that you are available, so my question is, Is it possible, I'm saying is it possible that you might reconsider your position, let's say somewhere along in March or April, in the late primaries, would you like to offset any negative connotations that might develop by complete absence of yourself from the primaries, would you reconsider?

MR. HUMPHREY: I have no plan to do so and that's a very honest answer as I've said to others. I recognize there is some validity to what you have to say as I think particularly people who are politically sensitive, writers, commentators, the people that make political news, might very well interpret my posture, my stand as he's just going to ride out the storm and hopefully things will work out for him and he's going to run off with the prize. I can't help what they figure out about me; I'm not a very conspiring fellow, that's one of my many weaknesses and I'm just going to do what I want to do.

It isn't going to break my heart if I'm not President of the United States. Of course, I wanted to be President. Of course I believe that any man who has been in public life as long as I have and to the depth that I've been, he would be deceiving you and deceiving himself if he didn't say that it would be the capping climax of his life to be President but I don't have the hunger for the Office as that once characterized my life and that is a fact. So I have come along pretty well and I decided I just don't worry about what people think about that. I really mean it. I don't know that that's being very smart or what it is, I know that I can go home to my home state and if I work hard and give a good accounting of myself, I believe that it's possible for me, better than a 50-50 chance, or at least a 50-50 chance to be reelected to the United States Senate. Now to me that would be very important, but even if I were not, I have no intention of looking for the highest cliff and jumping off.

I have had a good life, I've gone through most things that everybody wanted to go through who's ever been in politics. I got close enough to the White House door to at last look through the keyhole and let me also say this, that at my time of life, with the background of experience that I believe I had which has been very exciting and demanding, I'd like to be free to call the shots as I see them. I don't see that they're all going to be right, because a man that talks as much as I do is bound to get into trouble. I know that, but I'd rather be in trouble talking than get in trouble doing nothing and that's a fact.

I'm an action man. A little too loquacious but I'm not about ready to change to please you now either, because I enjoy what I'm saying. Now every primary becomes almost like a state election. You get down to Florida and all at once you've got to kind of lean with the breezes of Florida. You get up to Wisconsin and you freeze with the blizzards of Wisconsin. And you get out to California and they're asking you about proposition this and proposition that and the first thing you know, you're being more parochial than you are being Presidential. I don't need that. I've been through the primaries, I went through primaries in 1972 and I won four of them in a row. It was hard for anybody to get the message but I won them. I never appeared on *Newsweek* or *Time,* even though I won Pennsylvania, Ohio, West Virginia, and Indiana, bang, bang, bang, bang. And I came in second in Florida after being there only two months while other candidates had been there a year. I got more popular votes than any other candidate in the primaries.

I've been on the political scene all of my life since 1945, people have heard me so much they don't need six months more of me out on the hustings. Plus the fact I got a job to do and I'll tell you what I honestly believe. I think the people today want us to stay on our job; I'm out here for the Joint Economic Commission Hearings. I have to process legislation this year; foreign assistance, military sales, military assistance, we're rewriting the legislation, we're not letting the Executive Branch run foot-loose and fancy-free with it. Grain inspection, scandal legislation, a national food policy, I have to take a report to the Budget Committees of the Congress on the President's budget as Chairman of the Joint Economic Committee. I have to review the Council on Economic Advisors' report. We have the 30th anniversary of the Employment Act. I've got five months of work that would literally stagger a bull. I don't need to add to it by going out in primaries.

You cannot be a good Senator and a good Presidential candidate at the same time. Now don't misunderstand me. I think a person has to make a choice, this is what I told my friend Senator Mondale; I said, "Fritz, if you're going to try to be a good Senator and a good Presidential candidate, you're going to fail." You've got to sacrifice a certain number of months in the Senate to be a good Presidential candidate. I don't say that's not worth it, as a matter of fact, it may be very well worth it, but I didn't want to do that this time and as I said to you, I think the country could get along without me. I can't get along without the country, I know that, but they can get along without me. But if my Party turns to me, I want to be prepared physically, emotionally, and every other way to be able to handle the issues that come and there's no better way I can do it than to be on the job thinking about them and calling the shots as I see them and I'd like to challenge this Administration a little bit too from a vantage point of not appearing like I'm looking for delegates. I don't need a thing, frankly; I don't need one thing except a lot of good life and good happiness. I've been blessed with good health recovery, I've got a nice home, I've got a good wife, got nine grandchildren, three sons and a daughter, that's all I can take care of, all I really need. Now you've got the message.

Index